The
Foundation
Series

Derek Prince

Volume Two

Book 3: From Jordan to
Pentecost

Book 4: Purposes of Pentecost

Sovereign World

Sovereign World Ltd
P.O. Box 17
Chichester
England PO20 6RY

The material in this book is an edited version of a radio
programme originally broadcast in the United States in
1963-4, under the title 'The Study Hour'.

This series was edited by Paul A. Ogle.

Typeset by M R Reprographics, 42 High Street, Chard,
Somerset TA20 1QS

Printed and bound in Great Britain by Cox & Wyman
Ltd, Reading

Volume Two ISBN 1 85240 006 4

The Foundation Series

VOLUME II:
Incorporating Books 3 & 4

Book 3

FROM JORDAN TO PENTECOST

"...for John truly baptised with water, but you shall be baptised with the Holy Spirit..." **Acts 1:5**

...the doctrine of baptisms... **Hebrews 6:2**

BOOK 3:
FROM JORDAN TO PENTECOST

TABLE OF CONTENTS

Chapter 1

THE VERB 'BAPTISE'

We are working our way systematically through the six great foundation doctrines of the Christian faith, as stated in **Hebrews 6:1-2.** The six doctrines there listed as the 'beginning' or 'foundation' of the doctrine of Christ are as follows:

1. *Repentance from dead works.*
2. *Faith toward God.*
3. *The doctrine of baptisms.*
4. *Laying on of hands.*
5. *Resurrection of the dead.*
6. *Eternal judgment.*

In Volume I, Book 2, we examined the first two of these six doctrines - that is, 'repentance from dead works' and 'faith toward God' - or more simply, 'repentance' and 'faith.' Now we shall move on to the third of these great foundation doctrines, 'the doctrine of baptisms.'

The logical way in which to begin this particular study is to discover, if possible, the correct, original meaning of the word 'baptism' - or, more accurately, of the verb 'to baptise,' from which the noun 'baptism' is formed.

Upon examination, this word 'baptise' proves to be a most unusual and interesting word. Actually it is not an English word at all. It is a pure Greek word, transliterated into letters of the English alphabet. If we write out the original Greek word in English letters, as accurately as it is possible to do, this gives us *'baptizo.'* Then, with the change of the final 'o' to an 'e,' we have the word in the form which has now become familiar - 'baptise.'

At this point someone may reasonably ask: 'Why was this particular word never translated? Why was it simply written over from Greek to English letters? Was it because the correct meaning of the original Greek word was not known, and therefore the translators did not know by what English word to translate it?'

No, this is definitely not the explanation. As we shall see in due course, the Greek word 'baptizo' has a perfectly definite and well-established meaning.

Root Meaning

In order to clear up the unusual circumstances connected with the use of this word 'baptise,' it is necessary to glance for a moment at the historical background of Bible translation.

By far the best known and the most influential of all the English translations of the Bible is that known as the 'King James Version' - the version which was translated and published through the authority of King James of Britain, in the early years of the seventeenth century. It is through this translation that the word 'baptise' has gained a place in the English language; and through this King James Version the word 'baptise' has been carried over into the great majority of all subsequent English versions of the Bible, as well as into a great many translations of the Bible that have been made into the languages of many different tribes and peoples in various parts of the world. Yet this word 'baptise,' both in its origin and in its form, is in fact completely alien to almost all those languages.

We may ask then: how did this unusual and unnatural form first find its way into the King James Version of the Bible?

The answer lies in the fact that King James, though holding political power as an absolute monarch, was answerable in matters of religion to the bishops of the established Church of England. Now the relationship between James and his bishops was not always too cordial, and James did not wish the new translation of the Bible, published in his name and with his authority, to make his relationship with his bishops any worse.

For this reason, he allowed it to be understood that, so

far as possible, nothing was to be introduced into the translation which would cause unnecessary offence to the bishops or which would be too obviously contrary to the practices of the established church. Hence, the Greek word *'baptizo,'* which could easily have become, in translation, a source of controversy, was never translated at all, but was simply written over direct into the English language.

In this connection, it is interesting to remark that the very word 'bishop' is another example of precisely the same influences at work. In actual fact, the word 'bishop' is no more an English word than the word 'baptise.'

'Bishop' is just another Greek word that has been taken over, without translation, into the English language; but in this case it has come by a slightly less direct route, by way of Latin. If the Greek original of the word 'bishop' had been translated everywhere it occurs in the New Testament by its natural and correct translation - which is 'overseer' - the resulting version could have been interpreted as a challenge to the hierarchical order of government that existed in the established Church of England. Therefore, in various places, the translators avoided the issue, and simply left the Greek word to stand in its anglicised form - 'bishop.'

However, let us now return to the word with which we are directly concerned in this study - the Greek word *'baptizo,'* and its English equivalent 'baptise.' This Greek verb *'baptizo'* is of a special, characteristic form of which there are a good many other examples in the Greek language. The characteristic feature of this verbal form is the insertion of the two letters 'iz' into a more simple, basic root. Thus, the simple, basic root is - *'bapto.'* The insertion into this root of the two extra letters - 'iz' - produces the compound form - *'baptizo.'* We find then that the simple, basic root is *'bapto.'* The compound form, produced from that root, is *'baptizo.'*

Now the insertion of the additional syllable, 'iz,' into any Greek verb produces a verb that has a special, causative meaning. That is to say, the compound verb thus formed always has the sense of **causing** something to be, or to happen. The precise nature of that which is thus caused to be, or to happen, is decided by the meaning of the simple root verb, out of which the compound, causative form has been built up.

With this in mind, we can now form a clear and accurate picture of the Greek verb *'baptizo.'* This is a compound, causative form, built up out of the simple, root form, *'bapto.'* Obviously, therefore, to get a proper understanding of *'baptizo,'* it is necessary first of all to ascertain the meaning of *'bapto.'*

Fortunately, there is no difficulty whatever in doing this. This simple root form *'bapto'* occurs three times in the Greek text of the New Testament which formed the basis of the English King James Version. In every one of these three instances the original Greek verb *'bapto'* is translated by the same English verb 'to dip.'

The three New Testament passages in which *'bapto'* occurs are as follows:

First, **Luke 16:24.** Here the rich man, in the torments of hell fire, cries out to Abraham:

> *'Father Abraham, have mercy on me, and send Lazarus that he may **dip** the tip of his finger in water and cool my tongue...'*

Second, **John 13:26.** Here, at the last supper, Jesus identifies the traitor, who is to betray Him, by giving His disciples a definite, distinguishing mark:

> *"It is he to whom I shall give a piece of bread when I have **dipped** it."*

Third, **Revelation 19:13.** Here John the Revelator describes the Lord Jesus Christ as he sees Him coming in glory, leading the avenging armies of heaven:

> *He was clothed with a robe **dipped** in blood...*

In all these three passages, both the English word used by the translators, and also the actual context of each passage, make it clear that the Greek verb *'bapto'* means, **'to dip something into a fluid and then take it out again.'**

In that standard work of Biblical reference - Dr Strong's 'Exhaustive Concordance of the Bible' - Dr Strong gives the following as the primary meaning of the verb *'bapto'*; 'to cover wholly with fluid' - hence, 'to dip.'

We also find in the New Testament a compound version of the verb *'bapto,'* formed by prefixing the Greek preposition *'en,'* or *'em'* - meaning 'in.' This gives the compound form *'embapto.'* This compound form, *'embapto,'* also occurs three times in the Greek text of the New Testament. The three passages are, **Matthew 26:23; Mark 14:20;** and **John 13:26.** Any student who cares to check for himself will quickly discover that in all these three passages this compound form *'embapto'* is translated, just like the simple form *'bapto,'* by the English verb 'to dip.'

We thus arrive at the following conclusion. The Greek verb *'bapto'* - either in its simple form, or with the prefix *'em'* meaning 'in' - occurs six times in the Greek text of the New Testament, and in every instance in the King James Version it is translated 'to dip.' In every instance, also, the context plainly indicates that the action described by this verb is that of **dipping something into a fluid, and then taking it out again.**

Having thus arrived with absolute definiteness at the correct meaning of the simple verb *'bapto,'* there is no difficulty whatever in going on from there to discover, with equal definiteness, the correct meaning of the causative compound form *'baptizo.'*

If *'bapto,'* means 'to dip something into a fluid, and then take it out again,' then *'baptizo'* can have only one possible, literal meaning. Logically, it must mean 'to cause something to be dipped into a fluid, and then taken out again.' More briefly, *'baptizo'* - from which we get the English word 'baptise' - means 'to cause something to be dipped.'

Historical Usage

This conclusion can be confirmed by tracing the word *'baptizo'* back into the earlier history of the Greek language.

In the third century before the Christian era the extensive conquests of Alexander the Great had had the effect of spreading the use of the Greek language far beyond the actual geographical confines of Greece herself, or even of the Greek cities and communities of Asia Minor. In this way, by the time of the New Testament, the Greek language had become the generally accepted medium of communication for most of the peoples in the lands bordering on the Mediterranean Sea.

It is this form of the Greek language which is found in the New Testament and which traces its origin, linguistically, back to the purer form of classical Greek originally used by the Greek cities and states in the preceding centuries. Thus most of the words used in New Testament Greek trace their origin and their meaning back to the earlier forms of classical Greek.

This is true of the word with which we are at present concerned - the verb *'baptizo.'* This word can be traced back into the earlier, classical form of the Greek language as far as the fifth century BC. From then on it has a continuous history in the Greek language right down into the first and second centuries AD (that is, throughout the whole period of the New Testament writings). Throughout this period of six or seven centuries, the word retains one unchanging basic meaning: 'to dip,' 'to plunge,' 'to submerge.' In this sense, it may be used either literally or metaphorically.

The following are some examples of its use throughout this period.

In the fifth or fourth century BC *'baptizo'* is used by Plato of a young many being **'overwhelmed'** by clever philosophical arguments.

In the writings of Hippocrates (attributed to the fourth century BC) *'baptizo'* is used of people being **'submerged'** in water, and of sponges being **'dipped'** in water.

In the Septuagint (the Greek version of the Old Testament attributed to the second or first century BC) *'baptizo'* is used to translate the passage, in **2 Kings 5:14,** where Naaman went down and **'dipped himself'** seven times in the Jordan.

In this passage *'baptizo'* is used in verse **14,** but a different Greek word is used in verse **10,** where the King James Version used 'wash.' In other words, *'baptizo'* means specifically to **'dip oneself,'** not merely to 'wash,' without dipping.)

Somewhere between 100BC and 100AD, *'baptizo'* is used by Strabo to describe people who cannot swim being **'submerged'** beneath the surface of water (in contrast to logs of wood which float on the surface).

In the first century AD *'baptizo'* is used by Josephus, metaphorically, to describe a man **'plunging'** a sword into his own neck, and of the city of Jerusalem being **'overwhelmed'** or **'plunged'** to irremediable destruction by internal strife. It is obvious that such metaphorical uses as these would not be possible, unless the literal meaning of the word was already clearly established.

In the first or second century AD *'baptizo'* is used twice by Plutarch to describe either the body of a person, or the figure of an idol, being **'immersed'** in the sea.

From this brief linguistic study it will be seen that the Greek word *'baptizo'* has always had one clear, definite meaning, which has never changed. From classical Greek right down into New Testament Greek it has always retained one and the same basic meaning: 'to cause something to be dipped' - 'to immerse something beneath the surface of water, or of some other fluid.' In most cases this act of immersion is temporary, not permanent.

I venture to say that any honest person, with adequate linguistic qualifications, who will thoroughly investigate this whole question, can come to only one conclusion: the correct meaning of the word *'baptizo'* both in the New Testament and elsewhere, is 'to cause something to be dipped.'

This brief analysis of the meaning of the word 'baptism' brings out two distinctive features which are found everywhere that this word is used in the New Testament. Every baptism, considered as an experience, is both 'total' and 'transitional.'

It is 'total' in the sense that it involves the whole person and the whole personality of the one being baptised; it is 'transitional' in the sense that, for the person being baptised, it marks a transition - a passing out of one stage or realm of experience, into a new stage or realm of experience, never previously entered into.

The act of baptism may thus be compared to the opening and closing of a door. The person being baptised passes through a door, opened up to him by the act of baptism, out of something old and familiar, into something new and unfamiliar; and thereafter the door is closed behind him, and there is no way of returning back through that closed door into the old ways and the old experiences.

Four Different Kinds Of Baptism

Bearing in mind this picture which we have formed of the nature of baptism, let us turn back once again to the passage where baptism is specified as one of the foundation doctrines of the Christian faith - that is, **Hebrews 6:2.** We observe that the word 'baptism' is here used in the plural, not in the singular. It is 'the doctrine of **baptisms'** (plural) - not 'the doctrine of baptism' (singular). This indicates plainly that the complete doctrine of the Christian faith includes more than one type of baptism.

Following this conclusion out through the pages of the New Testament, we discover that there are actually **four** distinct types of baptism referred to at different points. If we set out these four types of baptism in chronological order, conforming to the order in which they are revealed in the New Testament, we arrive at the following outline.

First, the baptism preached and practised by John the Baptist - a baptism in water - is directly connected with the message and experience of 'repentance.' This type of baptism is described in **Mark 1:4:**

John came baptising in the wilderness and preaching a baptism of repentance for the remission of sins.

Second, there is a type of baptism which is not precisely described by any one word in the New Testament, but which we may call the baptism of 'suffering.' This baptism is referred to by Jesus in **Luke 12:50:**

"But I have a baptism to be baptised with, and how distressed I am till it is accomplished!"

It is also referred to in **Mark 10:38.** This passage records a request made by the sons of Zebedee to have the privilege of sitting with Christ on His right hand and on His left

14

hand in His glory. To this request Jesus replied with the following question:

> "...You do not know what you ask. Can you drink the cup that I drink, and be baptised with the baptism that I am baptised with?"

It is plain that Jesus here refers to the spiritual and physical surrender that lay ahead of Him as He trod the path to the cross - the surrender of His whole being - spirit, soul and body - to the appointed will of the Father that He might take upon Himself the guilt of the world's sin and then pay by His vicarious sufferings the price required to expiate that sin. By these words Jesus indicated to His disciples that the fulfilment of His plan for their lives would in due course demand of them also a like total surrender of their whole being into the hands of God - even, if need be, for the suffering of death.

The third type of baptism revealed in the New Testament is Christian baptism in water. This is referred to by Christ in **Matthew 28:19,** where He says to His disciples:

> "Go therefore and make disciples of all nations, baptising them in the name of the Father and of the Son and of the Holy Spirit..."

The primary feature which thus distinguishes Christian baptism from the baptism of John the Baptist is that Christian baptism is to be carried out in the full name and authority of the Triune God - Father, Son, and Holy Spirit. This was not so with John's baptism.

The fourth type of baptism revealed in the New Testament is the baptism in the Holy Spirit. In **Acts 1:5,** Jesus speaks about this baptism, and carefully distinguishes it from baptism in water. He says to His disciples:

> "...for John truly baptised with water, but you shall be baptised with the Holy Spirit not many days from now."

Although in the New King James Version the preposition used is 'with' - baptised 'with' the Holy Spirit, in the actual Greek text the preposition used is 'in' - baptised 'in' the Holy Spirit. Throughout the entire Greek text of the New Testament there are only two prepositions used with the verb 'to baptise.' These are 'in' and 'into.' This is in full accord with our conclusion as to the literal meaning of the word 'baptise' - 'to cause to be dipped, or immersed.'

In **Acts 1:8,** Jesus reveals the basic purpose of the baptism in the Holy Spirit. He says:

"But you shall receive power when the Holy Spirit has come on you; and you shall be witnesses to me..."

Primarily, therefore, the baptism in the Holy Spirit is a supernatural enduement with power from on high to be a witness for Christ.

Of the four types of baptism which we have listed, there is one - the baptism of suffering - which belongs to a more advanced level of spiritual experience than the rest, and therefore does not come within the scope of this series of studies, which is deliberately limited to the basic doctrines and experiences of the Christian faith. For this reason, we shall say nothing more about this baptism of suffering, but we shall confine our attention to the other three types of baptism; and we shall deal with these in the order in which they are unfolded in the record of the New Testament: first, the baptism of John the Baptist; second, Christian baptism in water; third, the baptism in the Holy Spirit.

Chapter 2

HOW JOHN'S BAPTISM DIFFERS FROM CHRISTIAN BAPTISM

There are probably many Christians who are not fully clear as to the difference between the baptism of John the Baptist on the one hand, and Christian baptism on the other. Therefore it is helpful to begin the study of these two forms of baptism by turning to **Acts 19:1-5;** where these two types of baptism are set side by side, and the important difference between them is clearly brought out:

> *And it happened, while Apollos was at Corinth, that Paul, having passed through the upper regions, came to Ephesus. And finding some disciples*
> *he said to them, "Did you receive the Holy Spirit when you believed?" And they said to him, "We have not so much as heard whether there is a Holy Spirit."*
> *And he said to them, "Into what then were you baptised?" So they said, "Into John's baptism."*
> *Then Paul said, "John indeed baptised with a baptism of repentance, saying to the people that they should believe on Him who would come after him, that is, on Christ Jesus."*
> *When they heard this, they were baptised in the name of the Lord Jesus.*

Here, in Ephesus, it would seem that Paul encountered a group of people who made themselves known to him as 'disciples.' At first, Paul took them to be disciples of Christ - that is, Christians - but on closer examination he discovered that they were only disciples of John the Baptist.

They had heard and accepted John's message of repentance, and the form of baptism that went with it, but they had hitherto heard nothing of the gospel message centring in the life, death and resurrection of Jesus Christ, or of the Christian form of baptism directly connected with the acceptance of the gospel message.

After Paul had explained the message of the gospel to them, these people accepted it, and were once again baptised - this time, the Scripture states, *in the name of the Lord Jesus.*

This incident shows clearly that the baptism of John and Christian baptism are absolutely distinct in their nature and their significance; and that, once John's ministry had closed and the gospel dispensation had been inaugurated, John's baptism was no longer accepted as being equivalent to, or a substitute for, Christian baptism. On the contrary, those who had only received John's baptism were required to be baptised again with full Christian baptism.

John's Baptism - Repentance And Confession

Mark 1:3-5 provides a summary of John's message and ministry, with its accompanying form of baptism:

"The voice of one crying in the wilderness:
Prepare the way of the LORD,
Make His paths straight."
John came baptising in the wilderness and preaching
a baptism of repentance for the remission of sins.
And all the land of Judea, and those from Jerusalem,
went out to him and were all baptised by him in the
River Jordan, confessing their sins.

In the providence of God, John's message and ministry served two special purposes. First, they prepared the hearts of the people of Israel for the advent and revelation of their long-awaited Messiah, Jesus Christ. Second, they provided a link between the dispensation of the law and the prophets, which was closed by John's own ministry, and the dispensation of the gospel, which was initiated about three years later as a result of the death and resurrection of Jesus Christ.

In fulfilling both these purposes of God, John's ministry was of necessity brief and temporary. It did not constitute in itself a dispensation, but merely a period of transition.

In his message and ministry, John made two main demands upon the people: first, repentance; second, public confession of sins. Those who were willing to meet these two conditions were thereafter baptised by John in the river Jordan, as a public testimony that they had repented of their past sins and that they were committing themselves henceforward to lead better lives.

Mark 1:4 states:

> *John came baptising in the wilderness and preaching*
> *a baptism of repentance for the remission of sins.*

More literally, John preached a baptism of repentance *into the remission of sins.* This agrees with a similarly literal rendering of **Matthew 3:11,** where John himself uses the two prepositions 'in' and 'into':

> *"I indeed baptise you in water into repentance..."*

We see then that John's baptism was *into* repentance and *into* remission of sins. It is therefore most important to establish the meaning of the preposition *into* when used in this way after the verb 'to baptise.'

Obviously it does not mean that those who were baptised by John only entered into the experience of repentance and forgiveness **after** they had been baptised. On the contrary, when many of the Pharisees and Sadducees came to John to be baptised, John refused to accept them and demanded that they produce evidence of a real change in their lives **before** he would baptise them. This is recorded in **Matthew 3:7-8:**

> *But when he saw many of the Pharisees and Sadducees*
> *coming to his baptism, he said to them, "Brood of*
> *vipers! Who has warned you to flee from the wrath to*
> *come?*
> *"Therefore bear fruits worthy of repentance..."*

In other words, John demanded of them: "Prove first by your actions that there has been a real change in your lives, before you ask me to baptise you."

This proves that John demanded, as we should naturally expect, that those who came to him for baptism should produce evidence in their lives of repentance and consequent remission of sins, before he would baptise them. Plainly,

19

therefore, the phrase 'baptism of repentance for the remission of sins' should not be taken as indicating that these two inward experiences of repentance and forgiveness only followed after the outward act of being baptised. Rather, it indicates - as the context makes plain - that the outward act of being baptised served as a visible attestation and confirmation that those being baptised had already passed through the experiences of repentance and forgiveness.

Thus, the act of baptism served as an outward seal, giving assurance of an inward transformation which had already taken place.

The clear understanding of this point is of great importance, because this phrase, 'to baptise into, or unto,' recurs in two subsequent passages of the New Testament - once in connection with Christian baptism in water, and once in connection with the baptism in the Holy Spirit - and in each case we must follow the same principle of interpretation as that already established in regard to John's baptism. However, we shall leave until later the detailed examination of these two subsequent passages.

To return to John's baptism. We may sum up its effects as follows. Those who sincerely met John's conditions enjoyed a real experience of repentance and forgiveness, which was expressed in lives changed for the better. However, these experiences were similar in character to the ministry of John which produced them - they were essentially transitional.

Those whom John baptised did not achieve the condition of abiding inward peace and victory over sin, made possible only through the full gospel message of Jesus Christ; but their hearts were prepared to receive and respond to the gospel message when it should be proclaimed.

Christian Baptism - Fulfilling All Righteousness

Let us now turn from the transitional to the permanent - from the baptism of John to full Christian baptism, ordained by Christ Himself as an integral part of the complete gospel message. The passage of Scripture which serves best to introduce Christian baptism is **Matthew 3:13-17,** which describes the baptism of Jesus Himself:

> *Then Jesus came to Galilee to John at the Jordan to be*
> *baptised by him.*
> *And John tried to prevent Him, saying, "I have need*
> *to be baptised by You, and are You coming to me?"*
> *But Jesus answered and said to him, "Permit it to be*
> *so now, for thus it is fitting for us to fulfil all*
> *righteousness." Then he allowed Him.*
> *Then Jesus, when He had been baptised, came up im-*
> *mediately from the water; and behold, the heavens were*
> *opened to Him, and He saw the Spirit of God descend-*
> *ing like a dove and alighting upon Him.*
> *And suddenly a voice came from heaven, saying, "This*
> *is My beloved Son, in whom I am well pleased."*

The first point which must be cleared up in connection with this account is that, although Jesus was baptised by John the Baptist, the form of baptism through which He passed was not at all on the same level as that of all the other people whom John baptised. As we have already pointed out, John's baptism made two main demands upon the people: repentance, and confession of sins.

However, Jesus had never committed any sins which He needed to confess, or to repent of. Hence, He did not need to be baptised by John in at all the same way as all the other people who came to John for baptism.

John himself clearly recognised this fact, for in the passage which we have just read - in **Matthew 3:14,** he says:

> *"I have need to be baptised by You, and are You coming*
> *to me?"*

However, Jesus answers in the next verse:

> *"Permit it to be so now, for thus it is fitting for us*
> *to fulfil all righteousness."*

In this answer of Jesus we find both the reason why Jesus Himself was baptised, and also the true significance of full Christian baptism, as distinct from the temporary form of baptism administered by John. Jesus was not baptised by John as the outward evidence that He had repented of His sins - because He had no sins to repent of. On the

21

contrary, as Jesus Himself explained, he was baptised in order that he might *fulfil* (or complete) *all righteousness.*

In this - as in many other aspects of His life and ministry - Jesus was deliberately and consciously establishing a standard of behaviour. By being baptised by John, He was setting an example and pattern of the baptism in which He desired Christian believers to follow Him.

This is in full accord with the words of the apostle in **1 Peter 2:21-22:**

> *For to this you were called, because Christ also suffered for us, leaving us an example, that you should follow His steps:*
> *"Who committed no sin,*
> *Nor was guile found in His mouth"...*

This confirms that which we have already said: Jesus was not baptised by John because He had repented of His sins. On the contrary, as Peter states, Jesus *'committed no sin, Nor was guile found in His mouth'*. But in being thus baptised, He left an example for all Christians, that they should follow His steps.

With this in mind, let us turn back to the reason which Jesus Himself gave for being baptised, as stated in **Matthew 3:15,** and let us examine His words in greater detail: *'thus it is fitting for us to fulfil all righteousness.'*

For the sake of the clearest possible understanding, let us divide up this reason into three sections: first the word *thus;* second the phrase, *'it is fitting';* third the concluding section, *'to fulfil all righteousness.'*

First, the word *thus,* or more plainly, 'in this manner.' By His example, Jesus established a pattern for the manner, or method, of baptism. Jesus was not baptised as an infant. **Luke 2:22** records that, while Jesus was still an infant, His parents *'brought Him to Jerusalem to present Him to the Lord.'* There is no thought or suggestion here of baptism. Jesus was not baptised until He had come to years of understanding, so that He knew at that time both what He was doing and the reason why He was doing it.

Then again, with further reference to the manner of

baptism, we read in the next verse, **Matthew 3:16:**

*Then Jesus, when He had been baptised, **came up immediately from the water**...*

By simple logic we deduce from this that in being baptised, Jesus first went down into, and then came up out of, the water. Taken in conjunction with the plain, literal meaning of the verb 'to baptise' (which we have already discussed), this leaves no reasonable room to doubt that Jesus permitted Himself to be wholly immersed beneath the waters of Jordan.

Let us move on now to the second section of the reason given by Jesus for being baptised: *it is fitting.* This phrase suggests that, for those who would follow Christ, being baptised is something fitting, something ordained of God. It is not exactly a legal commandment, such as those imposed upon Israel by the law of Moses, but it is, for Christians, a most natural and becoming expression of sincere and wholehearted discipleship.

By using the plural form 'us' - *'it is fitting for us'* - it would seem that Jesus by anticipation identified Himself with all those of His believing people who would subsequently follow Him through this appointed act of faith and obedience.

Finally, we come to the concluding section: *'to fulfil* (or complete) *all righteousness.'* As we have already pointed out, Jesus did not go through the ordinance of baptism as evidence that He had confessed and repented of His sins. On the contrary, He had never committed any sins; He was always perfectly righteous. This righteousness was, in the first instance, an inward condition of heart which Jesus had always possessed.

However, in allowing Himself to be baptised, Jesus fulfilled - or completed - this inward righteousness by an outward act of obedience to the will of His heavenly Father; and it was through this outward act of obedience and dedication to God that He actually entered into the active life of ministry by which He fulfilled the plan of God the Father.

So it is with all true, believing Christians who are baptised. Such believers are not baptised merely because they

23

are sinners who have confessed and repented of their sins. This would be to place Christian baptism right back on the same level as John's baptism. It is true that Christians have confessed and repented of their sins. Without this, they could not be Christians at all. But they have passed beyond this into something much fuller and greater than was ever possible for those who knew only the message and the baptism of John.

Romans 5:1 tells us:

Therefore having been justified by faith, we have peace with God through our Lord Jesus Christ.

True Christians have not merely confessed and repented of their sins. They have done this, and more. By faith in the atoning death and resurrection of Jesus Christ on their behalf, they have been justified - they have been made righteous - the righteousness of Christ Himself has been imputed to them by God on the basis of their faith.

This is the reason why they are then baptised - not simply as evidence that they have confessed and repented of their sins - but in order *'to fulfil* (to complete) *all righteousness.'* By this outward act of obedience they complete the inward righteousness which they have already received in their hearts by faith.

This explanation shows us how totally different in its true nature and significance Christian baptism is from the baptism which John preached. We can now understand why the apostle Paul would not accept John's baptism for those who desired to be true Christians. Instead, he first instructed them in the full truth of the gospel centring in Christ's death and resurrection, and then insisted on their being baptised once again with full Christian baptism.

In conclusion, let us sum up the nature of Christian baptism. It is an outward act of obedience by which the believer fulfils, or completes, the inward righteousness which he already enjoys in his heart through faith in Christ's atoning death and resurrection.

Chapter 3

CONDITIONS FOR CHRISTIAN BAPTISM

We shall now go on to examine in detail and in logical order the exact conditions which must be fulfilled by those who desire to receive Christian baptism.

Repenting

The first condition is stated in **Acts 2:37-38,** which records the reaction of the Jewish multitude to Peter's sermon on the day of Pentecost, and the instructions which Peter proceeded to give them:

> *Now when they heard this, they were cut to the heart, and said to Peter and the rest of the apostles, "Men and brethren, what shall we do?"*
> *Then Peter said to them, "Repent, and let every one of you be baptised in the name of Jesus Christ for the remission of sins; and you shall receive the gift of the Holy Spirit."*

Here in answer to the question, *what shall we do?* the apostle Peter gives two clear and definite commands: first, repent; then, be baptised.

We have already seen (in Book 2) that repentance is the first response that God requires from any sinner who desires to be saved. Repentance, therefore, must precede baptism. Thereafter, baptism is the outward seal, or affirmation, of the inward change that has already been produced by repentance.

Believing

The second condition for Christian baptism is stated by Christ Himself, in **Mark 16:15-16:**

*And He said to them, "Go into all the world and preach
the gospel to every creature.
"He who believes and is baptised will be saved; but he
who does not believe will be condemned."*

Here Christ states that everywhere the gospel is
preached, those who desire to be saved are required to do
two things: first, to believe; then to be baptised.

This condition for baptism is illustrated in the encounter
between Philip and the Ethiopian eunuch, recorded in **Acts
8:26-39.** Here we read how Philip encountered the eunuch
on the road from Jerusalem to Gaza; heard him read from
the prophet Isaiah; went up and joined him in his chariot;
and then preached to him the gospel message of Christ's
suffering, death and resurrection, prophetically foreshown
by the prophet Isaiah. After some time, as they continued
together on their journey, their way led past some water;
and upon the eunuch's request, and profession of faith,
Philip there baptised him.

The actual incident of the eunuch's baptism is related
in **Acts 8:36-38:**

*Now as they went down the road, they came to some
water. And the eunuch said, "See here is water. What
hinders me from being baptised?"
Then Philip said, "If you believe with all your heart,
you may." And he answered and said, "I believe that
Jesus Christ is the Son of God."
So he commanded the chariot to stand still. And both
Philip and the eunuch went down into the water, and
he baptised him.*

We see here how the practice of the early church was
in full accord with the commandments of Christ. Christ said:
'He who believes and is baptised will be saved...' Philip said to
the eunuch: *'If you believe with all your heart, you may...'* -
be baptised. The eunuch replied: *'I believe that Jesus Christ
is the Son of God.'* We see therefore that a person who desires
Christian baptism must first confess faith in Jesus Christ as
the Son of God.

These first two requirements for baptism - repenting and
believing - line up directly with the first three foundation

doctrines presented in **Hebrews 6:1-2:** first, repentance; second, faith; third, the doctrine of baptisms. In experience, as in doctrine, baptism must be built upon repenting and believing.

A Good Conscience

A third condition for Christian baptism is stated by the apostle in **1 Peter 3:21.** Here Peter is comparing the ordinance of Christian baptism in water to the experience of Noah and his family, who were saved from the wrath and judgment of God when they entered by faith into the ark. Then, once within the ark, they passed safely through the waters of the flood. In direct reference to this experience of Noah and his family, Peter says:

> There is also an antitype which now saves us, namely baptism (not the removal of the filth of the flesh, but the answer of a good conscience towards God), through the resurrection of Jesus Christ...

Here Peter first dismisses the crude suggestion that the purpose of Christian baptism is any kind of cleansing, or bathing, of the physical body. Rather, he says, the essential condition of Christian baptism lies in the inner response of the believer's heart - 'the answer of a good conscience towards God.' This inner response of a good conscience towards God, Peter indicates, is made possible through faith in the resurrection of Jesus Christ.

We may briefly summarise the grounds upon which the Christian believer at his baptism may answer to God for his conduct with a good conscience. First, such a believer has humbly acknowledged his sins; second, he has confessed his faith in the death and resurrection of Christ as the necessary propitiation for his sins; third, by the outward act of obedience in being baptised he is completing the final requirement of God needed to give him the scriptural assurance of salvation. Having thus met all God's requirements for salvation, he is able to answer God with a good conscience.

27

Becoming A Disciple

The first three conditions for baptism - repenting, believing, and the answer of a good conscience - are summed up by a fourth requirement: becoming a disciple. In **Matthew 28:19-20** Christ commissions His apostles to carry the message of the gospel to all nations:

> *"Go therefore and make disciples of all the nations, baptising them in the name of the Father and of the Son and of the Holy Spirit,*
> *"teaching them to observe all things that I have commanded you..."*

Here making disciples, which precedes baptising, consists in bringing those who hear the gospel through the first three stages of repenting, believing and a good conscience. This makes new believers eligible for baptism, by which act they commit themselves publicly to a life of discipleship.

After this public act of commitment, those who have been baptised need to receive further, more thorough and more extensive teaching, in order that they may become true disciples - strong, intelligent, responsible Christians.

We may now sum up the scriptural requirements for baptism. The person who is to be baptised must first have heard enough of the gospel to understand the nature of his act. Then he must have repented of his sins; he must confess his faith that Jesus Christ is the Son of God; he must be able to answer God with a good conscience, on the grounds that he has fulfilled all God's requirements for salvation. Finally, he must commit himself to a life of discipleship.

We conclude, therefore, that to be eligible for Christian baptism acording to the New Testament standard a person must be able to meet these four conditions; and conversely, that any person who is not able to meet these conditions is not eligible for baptism.

Are Infants Eligible?

It will be seen immediately that these four conditions listed above for baptism automatically rule out one class of

28

persons - and that is infants. By its very nature, an infant cannot repent, cannot believe, cannot answer with a good conscience to God, and cannot become a disciple. Therefore, an infant cannot be eligible for baptism.

Now it is sometimes suggested that there are instances in the New Testament where whole families, or households, were baptised together; and that it is at best probable, if not definitely established, that infant members of these households were included with the rest in the act of baptism. Since this has an important bearing on the whole nature and purpose of baptism, it is desirable to investigate this suggestion with care.

The two households usually mentioned in connection with this suggestion are the household of Cornelius, in **Acts 10,** and the household of the Philippian jailer, in **Acts 16.**

Let us consider first the household of Cornelius. In **Acts 10:2,** we are told that Cornelius was *'a devout man and one who feared God with all his household...'* - that is, all the members of his household were God-fearing people. In verse **33** of the same chapter, Cornelius says to Peter, before the latter begins to preach:

> *"...Now therefore, we are all present before God, to hear all the things commanded you by God."*

This indicates that all those present were capable of hearing Peter's message.

In verses **44-46** of the same chapter we read how the Holy Spirit fell upon all those present:

> *While Peter was still speaking these words, the Holy Spirit fell upon all those who heard the word.*
> *And those of the circumcision who believed were astonished, as many as came with Peter, because the gift of the Holy Spirit had been poured out on the Gentiles also.*
> *For they heard them speak with tongues and magnify God.*

This indicates that all those present were capable not merely of hearing Peter's message, but also of receiving the Holy Spirit by faith, as a result of that message, and of speaking with other tongues. In fact, it was upon this very

29

ground that Peter accepted them as being eligible for baptism, for in verses **46-47** we read:

> *Then Peter answered,*
> *"Can anyone forbid water, that these should not be baptised who have received the Holy Spirit just as we have?"*

Furthermore, in the next chapter - **Acts 11** - when Peter gives to the apostles and brethren in Jerusalem an account of what had taken place in the house of Cornelius, he adds one further important fact concerning all the members of the household of Cornelius. In **Acts 11:12-14,** he describes how he was received by Cornelius into his house:

> *"...Moreover these six brethren accompanied me, and we entered the man's house.*
> *And he told us how he had seen an angel standing in his house, who said to him, 'Send men to Joppa, and call for Simon whose surname is Peter,*
> *who will tell you words by which you and all your household will be saved.'"*

We learn from this that, as a result of Peter's preaching in the house of Cornelius, every member of the household of Cornelius was saved.

If we now put together the various pieces of information that we have gleaned concerning the household of Cornelius, we arrive at the following facts actually stated about them: all of them were God-fearing; all of them heard Peter's message; all of them received the Holy Spirit and spoke with other tongues; all of them were saved. It is clear therefore that all of these were people capable of meeting the New Testament conditions for baptism; and that there were no infants among them.

Let us now move on to **Acts 16,** which is the other passage where the New Testament records the baptism of a whole household at one time. The household is that of the Philippian jailer. As a result of the miraculous earthquake that opened the prison doors and freed Paul and Silas and the other prisoners, the jailer was brought under deep fear and conviction, and desired to know the way of salvation. The incident of the jailer's salvation, and of the baptism of his whole household, is recorded in **Acts 16:29-34:**

> *Then he* (the jailer) *called for a light, ran in, and fell down trembling before Paul and Silas.*
> *And he brought them out and said, "Sirs, what must I do to be saved?"*
> *So they said, "Believe on the Lord Jesus Christ, and you will be saved, you and your household."*
> *Then they spoke the word of the Lord to him and to all who were in his house.*
> *And he took them the same hour of the night and washed their stripes. And immediately he and all his family were baptised.*
> *Now when he had brought them into his house, he set food before them; and he rejoiced, having believed in God with all his household.*

If we study this account carefully, we find that the jailer and the members of his household all shared together in three experiences: in verse **32,** we read that Paul and Silas *spoke the word of the Lord to him and to all who were in his house* - that is, all the members of his household heard the message of the gospel. In verse **33,** we read that the jailer was baptised, *he and all his family* - that is, all the members of his household were baptised. In verse **34,** we read that the jailer *rejoiced, having believed in God with all his household* - that is, all the members of his household believed in God.

From this we learn that not merely were all the members of the jailer's household baptised, but all of them also heard and believed the message of the gospel. This shows us that all were capable of meeting personally the New Testament conditions for baptism; and that there were no infants among them.

Neither in the household of Cornelius, nor in the household of the Philippian jailer, nor anywhere else in the New Testament is there any suggestion that infants were ever considered eligible for baptism.

Preliminary Instruction

Although is is most necessary to emphasise the

various conditions which those desiring Christian baptism must meet, we must also be careful in this connection to guard against an overemphasis on 'teaching,' which leads to unscriptural results. In some places - particularly in certain foreign mission fields - it is the established practice to insist that all those who present themselves for baptism are first subjected to a prolonged period of instruction, extending over weeks or months, before they are accepted for baptism. This practice is traced back to the words of Christ in **Matthew 28:19-20:**

> *"Go therefore and make disciples of all nations, baptising them in the name of the Father and of the Son and of the Holy Spirit,*
> *teaching them to observe all things that I have commanded you..."*

This emphasis on preliminary teaching is partly due to the fact that in the 1611 King James Version Christ's words are translated: *"Go therefore and **teach** all nations..."* However, the modern version, *"Go...and **make disciples**..."* is more accurate.

Let it be granted, however, that those desiring to be baptised must be taught first. The question is: how long does this preliminary process of teaching need to take? Should the time required be measured in months, in weeks, in days, or in hours?

In **Acts 2:41** we read the following conclusion to the events of the day of Pentecost:

> *Then those who gladly received his* (Peter's) *word were baptised; and that day about three thousand souls were added to them.*

The three thousand people whose baptism is here recorded had been a few hours previously open unbelievers, who rejected the claim of Jesus of Nazareth to be either the Messiah of Israel or the Son of God. From the end of Peter's sermon to the moment of their being baptised, the time required by the apostles to give them the necessary instruction could not have exceeded a few hours.

Acts 8:12 records the response of the people of Samaria to the preaching of Philip:

But when they believed Philip as he preached the things concerning the kingdom of God and the name of Jesus Christ, both men and women were baptised.

No exact period of time for instruction is here specified. As on the day of Pentecost, it could have been just a few hours. Certainly it could not have exceeded a few days, or a week or two at the very most.

A little further on in **Acts 8:36-39,** we read how Philip baptised the Ethiopian eunuch on the very same day that he first met him and preached the gospel to him. Here again, the period could not have exceeded a few hours.

Acts 9:17-18 describes how the disciple Ananias was directed by God to go to Saul of Tarsus and lay hands on him and pray for him. The record continues:

Immediately there fell from his (Saul's) *eyes something like scales, and he received his sight at once; and he arose and was baptised.*

Later, in **Acts 22:16,** Paul himself relates that Ananias said to him at this time:

'And now why are you waiting? Arise and be baptised...'

We see then that Saul of Tarsus - later Paul - was baptised on what was probably the actual day of his conversion - certainly within three days of the first revelation of Jesus Christ to him upon the Damascus road.

In **Acts 10:48** we read that Peter commanded Cornelius and his household to be baptised on the same day that he had first preached the gospel to them and the Holy Spirit had fallen upon them all.

In **Acts 16:14-15** we read how the Lord opened the heart of Lydia, the seller of purple, to the message of the gospel, and how she was then baptised, with all her household. In this case, no further details are given, and no exact period of time is specified.

In **Acts 16:33** we read how the Philippian jailer and all his household were baptised the very same night in which they first heard the gospel.

In these passages we have examined seven instances of the baptism of new converts. In every case, some measure of instruction was given first. Thereafter, in the majority of these cases, baptism followed within a few hours of conversion. In no case was baptism ever delayed more than a few days.

We are thus able to arrive at a clear picture of the practice of the early church in relation to baptism. Before baptism they presented the simple basic facts of the gospel, centring in the person of Christ, and in His life, death, and resurrection; and they related these facts to the act of baptism.

Baptism then followed immediately - normally, within a few hours - at the most, within a few days.

Finally, after baptism the new converts continued to receive the further, more detailed instruction which was needed to establish them firmly in the Christian faith. This latter phase of instruction is summed up in the verse in **Acts 2** which immediately follows the account of the baptism of the new converts - that is, **Acts 2:42:**

> *And they* (that is those who had been baptised)
> *continued steadfastly in the apostles' doctrine and*
> *fellowship, in the breaking of bread, and in prayers.*

This is the New Testament pattern for establishing new converts in the faith, after they have been baptised.

Chapter 4

SPIRITUAL SIGNIFICANCE OF CHRISTIAN BAPTISM

In this chapter we shall complete our examination of Christian baptism by unfolding, from the teaching of the New Testament, the spiritual significance of this ordinance.

How God's Grace Operates

The key text, which unlocks this truth, is found in **Romans 6:1-7**:

> *What shall we say then? Shall we continue in sin that grace may abound?*
> *Certainly not! How shall we who died to sin live any longer in it?*
> *Or do you not know that as many of us as were baptised into Christ Jesus were baptised into His death?*
> *Therefore we were buried with Him through baptism into death, that just as Christ was raised from the dead by the glory of the Father, even so we also should walk in newness of life.*
> *For if we have been united together in the likeness of His death, certainly we also shall be in the likeness of His resurrection,*
> *Knowing this, that our old man was crucified with Him, that the body of sin might be done away with, that we should no longer be slaves of sin.*
> *For he who has died has been freed from sin.*

In the previous chapter Paul has emphasised the abundance of God's grace towards the depths of man's sin, summed up in **Romans 5:20**:

> *...But where sin abounded, grace abounded much more.*

35

This naturally leads on to the question which Paul proceeds to ask in **Romans 6:1:** *What shall we say then? Shall we continue in sin that grace may abound?* In other words, Paul imagines someone asking: 'If God's grace is in proportion to man's sin, abounding most where sin abounds most, shall we deliberately go on sinning, that God's grace may abound toward us all the more? Is this the way to avail ourselves of God's grace toward sinners?'

Paul's answer to this very dangerous suggestion is that it is based on a complete misunderstanding of the way in which the grace of God operates. In order for a sinner to avail himself of God's grace, there must be a definite, personal transaction, by faith, between the sinner and God; and the nature of this transaction is such that it produces a total transformation within the personality of the sinner himself.

There are two opposite, but mutually complementary, sides to this transformation produced by God's grace in the sinner's personality. First, there is a death - a death to sin, and the old life. Then, there is a new life - a life lived to God and to righteousness.

In the light of this fact about the way in which God's grace operates in the sinner, and the results which it produces, we are faced with two alternative, mutually exclusive possibilities: if we have availed ourselves of God's grace, we are, as a necessary consequence, dead to sin; on the other hand, if we are not dead to sin, then we have not availed ourselves of God's grace. It is therefore illogical, and impossible, to speak of availing ourselves of God's grace and at the same time living in sin. These two things can never go together.

Paul points this out in **Romans 6:2:**

> *Certainly not! How shall we who died to sin live any longer in it?*

Just what are we to understand by this phrase, *died to sin*? To form a picture of this, let us imagine the case of a man who has been an outstanding sinner. Let us suppose that he has been habitually unkind and brutal to his wife and children; he has forbidden all mention of God or of religion in his home; he has used foul and blasphemous language; he has been a slave of alcohol and tobacco.

Now let us suppose that this man dies suddenly of a heart attack, sitting in his chair at home. On the table by him there is a lighted cigarette in the ashtray, and a glass of whiskey just poured out. Neither the cigarette nor the whiskey any longer produce any reaction from the man; there is no inward stirring of desire, no outward motion of his arm toward them. Why not? The reason is simple: the man is dead - dead to alcohol and dead to tobacco alike.

A little later his wife and children come back from the Sunday evening service at the local Gospel Tabernacle, singing the new gospel choruses that they have just learned. There is no reaction from the man - no anger, no violence, no blasphemous words. Why not? The reason is simple: the man is dead - dead to anger and dead to blasphemy alike.

In one short phrase, that man is *dead to sin.* Sin no longer has any attraction for him; sin no longer produces any reaction from him; sin no longer has any power over him.

This is the picture that the New Testament paints of the man who has availed himself, by faith, of God's grace toward the sinner. Through the operation of that grace, that man has become dead to sin. Sin no longer has any attraction for him; sin no longer produces any reaction from him; sin no longer has any power over him. Instead, he is alive to God and to righteousness.

Crucified And Resurrected With Christ

This fact, that the true Christian believer is, through God's grace, dead to sin, is stated repeatedly and emphatically throughout the New Testament.

For example, in the verses already quoted from **Romans 6:6-7:**

> *...knowing this, that our old man was crucified with Him* (Christ), *that the body of sin might be done away with, that we should no longer be slaves of sin.*
> *For he who has died has been freed* (or justified) *from sin.*

The meaning here is plain: for each person who has accepted the atoning death of Christ on his behalf, the old man - the old corrupt, sinful nature - is crucified; the body of sin has been done away with; through death, that person has been freed - or justified - from sin. There is no longer any need to be the slave of sin.

A little further on in the same chapter, verses **11, 12** and **14,** Paul repeats this teaching, with renewed emphasis:

> *Likewise you also, reckon yourselves to be dead indeed to sin, but alive to God in Christ Jesus our Lord.*
> *Therefore do not let sin reign in your mortal body, that you should obey it in its lusts...*
> *For sin shall not have dominion over you, for you are not under law but under grace.*

Again, the meaning is plain: as Christians, we are to reckon ourselves as being dead to sin, through the grace of God in Jesus Christ. As a result, there is no reason why sin should continue to exercise any control or dominion over us.

Further on, in **Romans 8:10,** Paul again states the same truth in the clearest and most emphatic way:

> *And if Christ is in you, the body is dead because of sin, but the Spirit is life because of righteousness.*

The words Paul uses *if Christ is in you* indicate that this truth applies to every true Christian believer in whose heart Christ dwells by faith. The double consequence of Christ indwelling the believer is, first, a death of the old carnal nature - *the body* (that is, the body of sin) *is dead;* second, a new life to righteousness through the operation of God's Spirit -*the Spirit is life because of righteousness.*

The apostle Peter presents the same truth with equal clarity in **1 Peter 2:24.** Speaking of the purpose of Christ's death upon the cross, he says:

> *...who Himself bore our sins in His own body on the tree, that we, having died to sins, might live for righteousness - by whose stripes you were healed.*

Peter, just like Paul, presents the two complementary aspects of the transformation that takes place within the believer who accepts the atoning death of Christ on his behalf: first, there is a death to sins; second, there is a living for righteousness. In fact, Peter states this as being the supreme purpose of Christ's death on the cross - *that we, having died to sins, might live for righteousness.*

The condition of being dead to sins and living to righteousness is something far beyond the mere forgiveness of past sins. In fact, it takes the true believer up into an altogether different realm of spiritual experience. The majority of professing Christians in almost all denominations have some kind of belief that their past sins can be forgiven. In fact, this is probably the main reason why they attend church - for the purpose of confessing, and obtaining forgiveness for, the sins which they have committed.

However, they have no thought or expectation of experiencing any inward transformation of their own nature. The result is that, having gone through some form of confessing their sins, they leave the church unchanged, to go out and continue committing the same kind of sins that they have been confessing. In due course, they are back in church again, confessing the same sins.

This is a man-made religion on the human level, to which some of the outward forms of Christianity have been attached. It has little or nothing in common with the salvation which God offers to the true believer through faith in Christ's atonement.

The central purpose of God in Christ's atonement was not simply that man should be able to receive forgiveness of his past sinful acts; but rather that, once having been forgiven for the past, he should be able to enter into a new realm of spiritual experience. Henceforth he should be dead to sins, but alive to God and to righteousness; he should no longer be the slave of sin; sin should no longer have any dominion over him.

This has been made possible because Christ, in His atonement, not merely took upon Himself the guilt of our sinful acts and then paid the full penalty for all those acts. Above and beyond this, Christ made Himself one with our corrupt, fallen, sinful nature; and when He died upon the cross, according to the plain statements of Scripture, that old nature of ours - 'our old man' - 'the body of sin' - died in Him, and with Him.

39

In order that the believer may enter into this, the full purpose of Christ's atonement, there are two simple, but essential conditions that must be fulfilled. These two conditions are stated by Paul, in their logical order, in **Romans 6.**

In **Romans 6:6,** Paul says:

> *...knowing this, that our old man was crucified with Him, that the body of sin might be done away with, that we should no longer be slaves of sin.*

Our old man being crucified with Him was a definite, historical event that occurred at a given moment in past time. In **Romans 6:11,** Paul says:

> *Likewise you also, reckon yourselves to be dead indeed to sin, but alive to God in Christ Jesus our Lord.*

Here the introductory word *likewise* points out the correspondence between the experience of Christ and the experience of the believer. The meaning is: 'Just as Christ died, so reckon that you also died with Him.' More briefly, 'Christ's death was your death.'

Here, then, are the two conditions for entering into this experience of being dead to sin and of living to righteousness and to God: first *knowing*; second *reckoning*. First, we must *know* what God's word teaches about the central purpose of Christ's death. Second, we must *reckon* God's Word to be true in our own particular case - we must apply this truth of God's Word by faith to our own condition. The experience can be ours only when, and only as long as, we thus *know*, and *reckon* as true, what God's Word teaches about the purpose of Christ's atonement.

Concerning this central purpose of Christ's atonement - *that we, having died to sins, might live for righteousness* we may make two statements which can scarcely be challenged. First, there is no truth of greater practical importance than this, contained in the whole revelation of the New Testament. Second, there is no truth about which greater ignorance, indifference, or unbelief prevail at the present time among professing Christians.

The root of this whole miserable condition lies in the word 'ignorance.' With good reason we may apply to this situation the words of the Lord in **Hosea 4:6:**

My people are destroyed for lack of knowledge.

The primary requirement stated by Paul for entering into the central purpose of Christ's atonement is, *knowing this.* If God's people do not know this truth, they cannot believe it; if they do not believe it, they cannot experience it. Therefore, the first great need is to bring this truth before the Church, and to keep it continually before the Church, in the clearest and most emphatic way.

First Burial, Then Resurrection

Now at this point it may be asked: 'What is the relationship between this central truth of Christ's atonement, and the ordinance of Christian baptism?' The answer to this question is very simple, and practical. In the natural realm, after every death there follows a burial. The same order applies also in the spiritual realm: first death, then burial. Through faith in Christ's atonement we reckon ourselves, according to God's Word, to be dead with Him - we reckon our old man, the body of sin, to be dead. Thereafter, the next act appointed by God's Word is the burial of this old man, this dead body of sin.

The ordinance by which we carry out this burial is the ordinance of Christian baptism. In every service of Christian baptism, carried out according to the pattern of the New Testament, there are two successive stages: first, a burial; second, a resurrection. These two stages of baptism correspond, exactly and perfectly, to the two stages of the inner transformation within the believer who accepts Christ's atonement on his behalf: first, the death to sin; second, the new life to righteousness and to God.

Christian baptism in water is, first, a burial in a typical grave of water; and second, a resurrection out of that grave into a new life that is lived to God and to righteousness. The burial is the outward expression of the *death to sin,* the *death of the old man;* the resurrection is the outward expression of the new life to righteousness and to God.

The New Testament explicitly declares this to be the true purpose and significance of Christian baptism.

In **Romans 6:3-4,** we read:

> *Or do you not know that as many of us as were baptised*
> *into Christ Jesus were baptised into His death?*
> *Therefore we were buried with Him through baptism*
> *into death, that just as Christ was raised from the dead*
> *by the glory of the Father, even so we also should walk*
> *in newness of life.*

Again, in **Colossians 2:12:**

> *...buried with Him in baptism, in which you also were*
> *raised with Him through faith in the working of God,*
> *who raised Him from the dead.*

In both these passages, the two successive stages of baptism are clearly set forth: first, we are buried with Christ by baptism - literally, immersion - into his death; second, we are raised up with Him, through faith in the working of God's power, to walk with Him in newness of life.

Apart from this basic truth of burial and resurrection, there are three other important facts about baptism contained in these verses.

First, by true Christian baptism we are baptised into Christ Himself - not into any particular church, or sect, or denomination. In agreement with this, Paul says in **Galatians 3:27:**

> *For as many of you as were baptised **into Christ** have*
> *put on Christ.*

There is no room here for anything less, or smaller, than Christ - Christ in His atoning death, and Christ in His triumphant resurrection.

Second, the effect of baptism depends upon the personal faith of the one being baptised; it is *through faith in the working of God* - more simply, 'through faith in what God does.' Without this faith, the mere ceremony of baptism alone is of no effect or validity whatever.

Third, the believer who is raised up out of the watery grave of baptism to walk in newness of life, does this not in his own power, but in the power of God's glory, the same power which raised Jesus Himself from the grave. In **Romans 1:4,** Paul reveals that the power which raised

Jesus from the grave was 'the Spirit of holiness' - that is, God's own Holy Spirit. Thus the believer who passes through the waters of baptism thereby commits himself to a new life to God and to righteousness, which is to be lived in total dependence upon the power of the Holy Spirit.

This agrees with what Paul says in **Romans 8:10** (the second part):

And if Christ is in you, the body is dead because of sin, but the Spirit is life because of righteousness.

God's Spirit alone can give the baptised believer the power that he needs for this new life of righteousness.

It is a general principle of educational psychology that children remember approximately forty percent of what they hear; sixty percent of what they hear and see; eighty percent of what they hear, see and do. In establishing the ordinance of Christian baptism in the church, God has applied this principle of psychology to the teaching of the great central purpose of Christ's atonement - *that we, having died to sins, might live for righteousness.*

According to the New Testament pattern, each time new believers are added to the church, they themselves act out, in the ordinance of baptism, their identification by faith with Christ first in His death and burial to sin, second in His resurrection to newness of life. In this way, the ordinance of baptism serves continually to bring and to keep before the whole church the great central purpose of Christ's atonement.

It follows that this vital truth concerning Christ's atonement can never be fully restored in the Christian church, until the true method and meaning of Christian baptism are first restored. Christian baptism must become once again, for each believer individually, and for the church as a whole, a re-enactment of this double truth - death and burial to sin, resurrection and life to righteousness and to God.

To complete this study, it remains to point out briefly that true Christian baptism does not produce within the believer this condition of *death to sin*, but rather it is the outward seal that the believer has already, by faith, entered into this condition. In the verses already quoted from **Romans 6,** Paul

43

states clearly that we are first dead with Christ to sin; and then after that we are baptised into Christ's death.

In this respect, Christian baptism is parallel to John's baptism. In John's baptism, the person to be baptised first repented of his sins, and after that he was baptised into repentance. In Christian baptism, the believer is first, by faith, dead with Christ to sin, and after that he is baptised into Christ's death. In each case the outward act of baptism does not in itself produce the inward spiritual condition; rather, it is the seal and affirmation that this inward condition has been produced already, by faith, in the heart of the person baptised.

Chapter 5

THE BAPTISM IN THE HOLY SPIRIT

Since the turn of the twentieth century, the subject of the baptism in the Holy Spirit has been arousing keen interest and discussion amongst ever widening circles of the Christian Church. Today it continues to be a theme of study, of discussion, and quite often of controversy, in almost all sections of Christendom. In view of this, we shall seek to approach this study in a way that is careful, thorough, and scriptural.

Seven New Testament References

First we shall enumerate the passages in the New Testament where the word 'baptise' is used in connection with the Holy Spirit. Appropriately enough - since 'seven' is distinctively the number of the Holy Spirit - there are seven such passages.

In **Matthew 3:11,** John the Baptist contrasts his own ministry with the ministry of Christ which is to follow, and he uses these words:

> *"I indeed baptise you with water unto* (into) *repentance, but He who is coming after me is mightier than I, whose sandals I am not worthy to carry. He will baptise you with the Holy Spirit and fire."*

Although the New King James Version here uses the English preposition 'with' in conjuction with the verb 'to baptise,' the actual preposition used in the original Greek is 'in.' This usage applies equally to baptising in water and to baptising in the Holy Spirit. In each case, the Greek preposition used is 'in.' In fact, the only prepositions ever used anywhere in the New Testament in conjunction with the verb 'to baptise' are 'in' and 'into.' It is unfortunate that the New King James Version, by using a variety of different prepositional forms, has obscured the clear teaching of the original text.

In **Mark 1:8,** the words of John the Baptist concerning Christ are rendered as follows:

> *"I indeed baptised you with water, but He will baptise you with the Holy Spirit."*

In each case, the Greek preposition used is 'in.'

In **Luke 3:16,** the words of John the Baptist are rendered as follows:

> *John answered, saying to them all, "I indeed baptise you with water; but One mightier than I is coming, whose sandal strap I am not worthy to loose. He will baptise you with the Holy Spirit and with fire."*

Here again, the literal translation is *in the Holy Spirit.*

In **John 1:33,** the testimony of John the Baptist concerning Christ is given as follows:

> *"I did not know Him, but He who sent me to baptise with water said to me, 'Upon whom you see the Spirit descending, and remaining on Him, this is He who baptises with the Holy Spirit.'"*

Again, in each case the Greek preposition used is 'in.'

In **Acts 1:5,** shortly before His ascension into heaven, Jesus says to His disciples:

> *"...for John truly baptised with water, but you shall be baptised with the Holy Spirit not many days from now."*

More literally, Jesus says: *"...you shall be baptised in the Holy Spirit..."*

In **Acts 11:16,** Peter is describing the events which took place in the household of Cornelius, and in this connection he quotes the actual words of Jesus as given in **Acts 1:5,** for he says:

> *"Then I remembered the word of the Lord, how He said, 'John indeed baptised with water, but you shall be baptised with* (literally in) *the Holy Spirit.'"*

Finally, in **1 Corinthians 12:13,** Paul says:

For by one Spirit we were all baptised into one body - whether Jews or Greeks, whether slaves or free - and have all been made to drink into one Spirit.

Here the New King James Version used the preposition 'by' - *by one Spirit we were all baptised into one body.* However, the preposition used in the original Greek text is 'in' - *in one Spirit we were all baptised into one body.* Thus, the usage of Paul in this passage is in perfect harmony with the usage of the Gospels and the book of Acts.

Unfortunately, the accident that the translators of the King James Versions - both Old and New - have used the phrase *by one Spirit* in this particular passage has given rise to some strange doctrines. It has been suggested that Paul is here referring to some special experience, different from that referred to in the Gospels or the book of Acts, and that in this special experience the Holy Spirit is Himself the agent who does the baptising. Had the authors of these doctrines paused long enough to consult the original Greek text, they would have found no basis there for any such doctrine. In fact, the whole teaching of the entire New Testament in this connection agrees in this fact, clearly and emphatically stated: Jesus Christ Himself alone - and no other - is the One who baptises in the Holy Spirit.

We must also add that Paul's usage here of the phrase 'baptised into,' in connection with the baptism in the Holy Spirit, agrees with the usage of the same phrase which we have already noted in connection with John's baptism and with Christian baptism in water. In both these cases we pointed out that the act of baptism was an outward seal and affirmation of an inward spiritual condition into which the person being baptised had already entered by faith. The same applies to Paul's statement here about the relationship between the baptism in the Holy Spirit and membership of the body of Christ. The baptism in the Holy Spirit does not make a person a member of the body of Christ. Rather, it is a supernatural seal, acknowledging that that person has already, by faith, become a member of Christ's body.

Let us now briefly summarise the lessons which we may learn from considering the above seven passages in the New Testament where the phrase *to baptise in the Holy Spirit* is used.

In six out of these seven passages, the experience of being baptised in the Holy Spirit is both compared, and contrasted, with being baptised in water.

In two out of the seven passages, *fire* is joined with *the Holy Spirit,* and the experience is described as *being baptised in the Holy Spirit and fire.*

Apart from the verb 'to baptise,' the only other verb used in these passages in connection with the Holy Spirit is the verb 'to drink.' In **1 Corinthians 12:13,** Paul says: ...*we have all been made to drink into one Spirit.* In modern English we should say more simply: 'We have all been given to drink of one Spirit.'

The use of the verb 'to drink' agrees with what Jesus Himself says concerning the Holy Spirit, in **John 7:37-39:**

> ...*Jesus stood and cried out, saying, "If anyone thirsts, let him come to Me and drink.*
> *"He who believes in Me, as the Scripture has said, out of his heart will flow rivers of living water."*
> *But this He spoke concerning the Spirit, whom those believing in Him would receive; for the Holy Spirit was not yet given, because Jesus was not yet glorified.*

Here Jesus speaks of an experience in which the believer is to receive the gift of the Holy Spirit through a process analogous to that of drinking water.

This in turn harmonises with the passage in **Acts 2:4,** concerning the disciples in the upper room on the day of Pentecost, where it states that *they were all **filled with** the Holy Spirit.*

It agrees also with various passages in the book of Acts which speak about believers **receiving** the Holy Spirit. For example, in **Acts 8:15** and **17,** concerning the Samaritans converted through the preaching of Philip, we read that the apostles Peter and John were later sent down to them from Jerusalem:

...who, when they had come down, prayed for them
that they might receive the Holy Spirit...
Then they laid hands on them, and they received the
Holy Spirit.

Again, in **Acts 10:47,** Peter says concerning the people
in the house of Cornelius upon whom the Holy Spirit had
just fallen:

"Can anyone forbid water, that these should not be bap-
tised who have received the Holy Spirit just as we
have?"

Further on, in **Acts 19:2,** Paul asks the disciples whom
he meets at Ephesus:

"Did you receive the Holy Spirit when you believed?"

In all these passages, the use of phrases such as 'to drink
of the Holy Spirit,' 'to be filled with the Holy Spirit,' 'to
receive the Holy Spirit,' suggests an experience in which
the believer receives the fulness of the Holy Spirit inwardly
within himself.

Immersion From Above

We have seen that the literal, root meaning of the
verb 'to baptise' is 'to cause something to be dipped, or
immersed.' Thus, the phrase 'to be baptised in the Holy
Spirit' suggests an experience in which the believer's whole
personality is immersed, surrounded, enveloped in the
presence and power of the Holy Spirit, coming down over
him from above and from without.

We need to bear in mind that, in the natural order, there
are two possible ways of being immersed in water. A person may go down beneath the surface of the water and come
up from under it. Alternatively, a person may walk under
a waterfall and allow himself to be immersed from above.
It is this second form of immersion of which the spiritual
counterpart is the baptism in the Holy Spirit.

In full accord with this picture of immersion, we find
that, without exception, in every place in the book of Acts
where the baptism in the Holy Spirit is described, language
is used which indicates that the Holy Spirit comes down

over, or is poured out upon, the believer from above.

For example, in **Acts 2:2,** we read that on the day of Pentecost,

> *...there came a sound from heaven, as of a rushing wind, and it filled the whole house where they were sitting.*

These words reveal that the Holy Spirit came down over these disciples from above and completely immersed and enveloped them, even to the extent of filling the whole house where they were sitting.

Further on in the same chapter, Peter twice confirms this interpretation of the experience. In **Acts 2:17,** he declares that this experience is the fulfilment of God's promise:

> *'...in the last days...I will pour out of My Spirit on all flesh...'*

And in verse **33,** he says again concerning Christ:

> *"Therefore being exalted to the right hand of God, and having received from the Father the promise of the Holy Spirit, He poured out this which you now see and hear."*

In each case the picture is one of the Holy Spirit being poured out over the believers from above.

In **Acts 8:16,** the phrase used for the same experience is that of the Holy Spirit 'falling upon' the believers. Here again, the language depicts the Spirit coming down over them from above.

In **Acts 10,** concerning the people in the house of Cornelius, both phrases are used one after the other. In verse **44** we read: *the Holy Spirit fell upon all those who heard the word.* In verse **45** we read: *the gift of the Holy Spirit had been poured out on the Gentiles also.* This shows that the phrases 'to fall upon' and 'to be poured out on' are used interchangeably in this connection.

Again, in **Acts 11:15,** Peter describes the same event in the house of Cornelius, and says:

> *"...the Holy Spirit fell upon them, as upon us at the beginning."*

Here the phrase, *as upon us at the beginning,* indicates that the experience of Cornelius and his household is in this respect exactly parallel to the experience of the disciples in the upper room on the day of Pentecost.

Finally, in **Acts 19:6,** we read concerning the disciples in Ephesus, after they had been baptised in water:

And when Paul had laid hands on them, the Holy Spirit came upon them...

Here the phrase 'to come upon' is obviously similar in meaning to the phrase used in previous passages, 'to fall upon.'

If we now seek to fit together the pictures, or impressions, created by the various phrases which we have found used in the New Testament, we arrive at a conclusion which may be summarised as follows.

The experience of which we are speaking is made up of two distinct, but complementary aspects, one outward, and the other inward.

Outwardly, the invisible, but absolutely real, presence and power of the Holy Spirit comes down from above upon the believer, and completely surrounds, envelops, and immerses him.

Inwardly, the believer, in the likeness of one drinking, receives the presence and power of the Holy Spirit within himself, until there comes a point at which the Holy Spirit, thus received, in turn wells up within the believer and flows forth like a river from the inmost depths of his being.

No human language can fully exhaust the various phases and aspects of a mighty, supernatural experience such as this, but it may perhaps be illuminating to borrow a picture from the Old Testament.

In the days of Noah we read that the whole world that then existed was submerged beneath the flood. In bringing about this flood, we read that God used two distinct, but complementary processes. In **Genesis 7:11,** we read the following account of how the flood was brought about:

In the six hundredth year of Noah's life, in the second month, the seventeenth day of the month, on that day all the fountains of the great deep were broken up, and the windows of heaven were opened.

This account reveals that the waters of the flood came from two sources: from within, *the fountains of the great deep*

51

were broken up; from above, *the windows of heaven were opened,* and the rain was poured down.

We must of course observe that the flood of Noah's day was a flood of divine wrath and judgment; the flood which immerses the New Testament believer is one of divine mercy, and glory, and blessing. However, with this qualification, the experience of the New Testament believer, who receives the fulness of the Holy Spirit, exhibits the same two aspects as in the account of Noah's flood: from within, the fountains of the great deep within the believer's own personality are broken up and there gushes out a mighty flood of blessing and power from his inmost being; from above, the windows of God's mercy are opened upon the believer, and from these opened windows there is poured upon him such a deluge of glory and blessing that his whole personality is immersed in its outpourings.

It must be emphasised that we are not here speaking of two separate experiences, but rather of two distinct, yet complementary aspects which together make up the fulness of one single experience.

Someone may object that it is difficult to understand how the believer can at one and the same time be filled with the Holy Spirit from within, and immersed in the Holy Spirit from without. However, such an objection in reality serves only to illustrate the limitations of human speech and understanding. An exactly similar type of objection might be brought against such statements as those made by Christ Himself, that He is in the Father and the Father in Him; or again, that Christ is in the believer, and the believer in Christ.

In the last resort, if men persist in caviling at a supernatural experience of this kind on the basis of human limitations of expression or understanding, the best and shortest answer is found in the words of the Scottish preacher, who said: 'It's better felt, than telt!'

The Outward Evidence

Up to this point we have considered the invisible, inward nature of the baptism in the Holy Spirit, as revealed by the words used in the New Testament to describe it. We must now go on to consider what are the outward manifestations which accompany this inward experience.

First of all, we must point out that it is perfectly scriptural to use the word 'manifestation' in connection with the Holy Spirit. We acknowledge of course that the Holy Spirit Himself is, by His very nature, invisible. In this respect, He is compared by Jesus to the wind. In **John 3:8,** Jesus says concerning the operation of the Holy Spirit:

> *"The wind blows where it wishes, and you hear the sound of it, but cannot tell where it comes from and where it goes. So is everyone who is born of the Spirit."*

Although the wind itself is invisible, the effects which the wind produces, when it blows, can in many cases be both seen and heard. For example, when the wind blows, the dust rises from the streets; the trees all bend in one direction; the leaves rustle; the waves of the sea roar; the clouds go flying across the sky. These effects produced by the wind can be seen, or heard.

So it is, Jesus says, with the Holy Spirit. The Spirit Himself is invisible. But the effects which the Holy Spirit produces, when He begins to work, can often be seen, or heard. This fact is confirmed by the language used by the New Testament in various places.

For example, in **Acts 2:33,** the apostle Peter refers to the effects produced by the descent of the Holy Spirit on the day of Pentecost, and he says:

> *"Therefore being exalted to the right hand of God, and having received from the Father the promise of the Holy Spirit, He (Christ) poured out this which you now* ***see and hear.****"*

Here *this* refers to the effects of the Holy Spirit at work, which, Peter says, can be both seen and heard.

Again, in **1 Corinthians 2:4,** Paul describes his own ministry in these words:

> *And my speech and my preaching were not with persuasive words of human wisdom, but in* ***demonstration*** *of the Spirit and of power...*

In **1 Corinthians 12:7,** Paul says:

*But the **manifestation** of the Spirit is given to each one for the profit of all.*

Notice the phrases which Paul uses in connection with the Holy Spirit - the *demonstration of the Spirit* and *the manifestation of the Spirit.* These two words *demonstration* and *manifestation* show clearly that the presence and operation of the Holy Spirit can produce effects which can be directly perceived by our physical senses.

With this in mind, let us now turn to the various passages in the New Testament where the baptism in the Holy Spirit is described - that is, where we are told what actually happened to the people who received this experience. Let us see what are the outward manifestations which accompany this operation of the Spirit.

There are actually three places in the New Testament where we are told what happened when people were baptised in the Holy Spirit. These are: **Acts 2:2-4; Acts 10:44-46;** and **Acts 19:6.**

We shall consider, in order, the actual words used in each of these three passages to describe what took place.

First, **Acts 2:2-4.** This is the record of what happened to the first disciples on the day of Pentecost:

And suddenly there came a sound from heaven, as of a rushing mighty wind, and it filled the whole house where they were sitting.
Then there appeared to them divided tongues, as of fire, and one sat upon each of them.
And they were all filled with the Holy Spirit and began to speak with other tongues, as the Spirit gave them utterance.

Second, **Acts 10:44-46.** This is the record of what happened when Peter first preached the gospel to Cornelius and his household:

While Peter was still speaking these words, the Holy Spirit fell upon all those who heard the word.
And those of the circumcision who believed were astonished, as many came with Peter, because the gift

*of the Holy Spirit had been poured out on the Gentiles
also.
For they heard them speak with tongues and magnify
God.*

Third, **Acts 19:6.** This describes what happened to the
first group of converts, to whom Paul preached at Ephesus:

*And when Paul had laid hands on them, the Holy Spirit
came upon them, and they spoke with tongues and
prophesied.*

If we now carefully compare these three passages, we
shall find that there is one - and only one - outward
manifestation which is common to all three occasions where
people received the baptism in the Holy Spirit. In each case,
the Scripture explicitly states that those who received this
experience *spoke with tongues* - or *spoke with other tongues.*

Other supernatural manifestations are also mentioned,
but none is mentioned as having taken place on more than
one of the three occasions.

For example, on the day of Pentecost there was the
sound of a rushing wind, and visible tongues of fire were
seen. However, these manifestations were not repeated on
the other two occasions.

Again, at Ephesus we read that the new converts not
only spoke in tongues, but also prophesied. However, this
manifestation of prophesying is not mentioned as having
taken place either on the day of Pentecost or in the house
of Cornelius.

The only manifestation which is common to all three
occasions is that all those who received the experience *spoke
with tongues.*

The apostle Peter and the other Jews, who already knew
what had taken place on the day of Pentecost, went to the
house of Cornelius reluctantly, against their own inclinations, under the explicit direction of God. At that time the
Jewish believers did not realise that the gospel was for the
Gentiles, or that Gentiles could be saved and become Christians. However, the moment that Peter and the other Jews
heard the Gentiles speak with tongues, they immediately
understood and acknowledged that these Gentiles had

received the Holy Spirit just as truly and as fully as the Jews themselves. They never asked for any additional evidence.

The Scripture says that they *were astonished...because the gift of the Holy Spirit had been poured out on the Gentiles also. For they heard them speak with tongues...* For Peter and the other Jews, the sole and sufficient evidence that the Gentiles had received the Holy Spirit was that they had heard them speak with tongues.

In the next chapter - **Acts 11** - we read that Peter was called to account by the other leaders of the church in Jerusalem for his conduct in visiting and preaching to Gentiles. In his own defence, he explained what had taken place in the house of Cornelius. In this connection, he says, in **Acts 11:15:**

> *"And as I began to speak, the Holy Spirit fell upon them, as upon us at the beginning."*

Thus Peter directly compares the experience which the household of Cornelius received with that which the first disciples received on the day of Pentecost - for he says, *as upon us at the beginning.* Yet in the house of Cornelius there was no mention of a mighty rushing wind, or tongues of fire. The one sufficient manifestation which set the divine seal upon the experience of Cornelius and his household was that they spoke with tongues.

From this we conclude that the manifestation of speaking with tongues, as the Holy Spirit gives utterance, is the accepted New Testament evidence that a person has received the baptism in the Holy Spirit. In confirmation of this conclusion, we may make the following statements.

First, this was the evidence which the apostles themselves received in their own experience.

Second, this was the evidence which the apostles accepted in the experience of others.

Third, the apostles never asked for any other alternative evidence.

Fourth, no other alternative evidence is offered to us anywhere in the New Testament.

In the next chapter we shall examine this conclusion

further; and we shall consider various criticisms, or objections, which are commonly raised against it.

Chapter 6

RECEIVE THE HOLY SPIRIT

A number of different objections are often raised against our conclusion that the manifestation of speaking with tongues is the accepted New Testament evidence that a person has received the baptism in the Holy Spirit. For the sake of clarity and thoroughness, therefore, it is necessary for us to consider some of the most common objections to this conclusion.

One standard objection takes the following form: every Christian who has had a genuine experience of conversion and salvation has automatically received the Holy Spirit in that experience, and therefore does not need any further experience, or any other evidence, in order to have the assurance of having received the Holy Spirit.

Much confusion and controversy concerning this issue will be avoided once we establish one important, scriptural fact: the New Testament depicts two different and separate experiences, both of which are described as 'receiving the Holy Spirit.' This means that it is possible for a Christian to have 'received the Holy Spirit' in one use of the expression, but not in the other.

The Pattern Of The Apostles

A simple way to distinguish these two experiences is to compare the events of two Sundays, each of which was uniquely important in the history of the Christian Church. The first is Resurrection Sunday; the second is Pentecost Sunday.

One main event of Resurrection Sunday is described in **John 20:22**. When Jesus appeared to the apostles in a group for the first time after His resurrection,

> ...He breathed on them, and said to them, "Receive the Holy Spirit."

The action of Jesus in breathing on the apostles was suited to the words which accompanied it: *"Receive the Holy Spirit."* In Greek the same word 'pneuma' means both 'spirit' and 'breath.' The words of Jesus could therefore be translated, "Receive Holy Breath." Furthermore, the tense of the imperative form 'Receive' indicated that the receiving was a single, complete experience which took place as Jesus uttered the word. It is therefore an incontestable, scriptural fact that at that moment the apostles did actually 'receive the Holy Spirit.'

In this first encounter with the resurrected Christ, the apostles passed from 'Old Testament salvation' to 'New Testament salvation.' Up to that time the believers of the Old Testament had looked forward by faith, through prophecies and types and shadows, to a redemptive act which had not yet taken place. Those who enter into 'New Testament salvation,' on the other hand, look back with clear vision to a single historical event: the death and resurrection of Christ. Their salvation is complete.

In **Romans 10:9** Paul states the two requirements for receiving this New Testament salvation:

> ...that if you confess with your mouth the Lord Jesus and believe in your heart that God has raised Him from the dead, you will be saved.

The two requirements are to confess Jesus as Lord and to believe that God raised Him from the dead. Prior to Resurrection Sunday the apostles had already confessed Jesus as Lord. But now, for the first time, they also believed that God raised Him from the dead. Thus their salvation was completed.

This was the point at which they experienced the new birth. The Holy Spirit breathed into them by Jesus imparted to them a totally new kind of life - eternal life - life which had triumphed over sin and Satan, over death and the grave.

This experience of the apostles stands as a pattern for

all who enter into the new birth. It contains two essential elements: a direct, personal revelation of the resurrected Christ; and the receiving of the Holy Spirit as divine, eternal life. This agrees with the words of Paul in **Romans 8:10:** *'...the Spirit is life because of righteousness'* - that is, the righteousness imputed to all who believe in Christ's death and resurrection.

Yet even after this wonderful encounter, Jesus made it plain to the apostles that their experience of the Holy Spirit was still incomplete. In His final words to them before His ascension, He commanded them not to go out and preach immediately, but to go back to Jerusalem and to wait there until they were baptised in the Holy Spirit and thus endued with power from on high for effective witness and service.

In **Luke 24:49,** Jesus says:

> *"Behold, I send the Promise of My Father upon you; but tarry in the city of Jerusalem until you are endued with power from on high."*

In **Acts 1:5,** He further explains:

> *"For John truly baptised with water, but you shall be baptised with the Holy Spirit not many days from now."*

And again, in **Acts 1:8:**

> *"But you shall receive power when the Holy Spirit has come upon you; and you shall be witnesses to Me..."*

Almost all interpreters of the Bible agree that this promise of being baptised in the Holy Spirit was fulfilled on Pentecost Sunday. The climax of the experience is described in **Acts 2:4:**

> *And they were all filled with the Holy Spirit and began to speak with other tongues, as the Spirit gave them utterance.*

It was on Resurrection Sunday that the apostles received the inbreathed Spirit from Christ and thus entered into salvation and the new birth. Yet it was not until Pentecost Sunday, seven weeks later, that they were baptised in - or filled with - the Holy Spirit. This shows that salvation, or the new birth, is a distinct and separate experience from the baptism in the Holy Spirit, although each of them is described as 'receiving the Holy Spirit.'

Later on Pentecost Sunday, in **Acts 2:33,** Peter explained that it was Christ, after His ascension, who had poured out the Holy Spirit on the waiting disciples:

> *"Therefore being exalted to the right hand of God, and having received from the Father the promise of the Holy Spirit, He poured out this which you now see and hear."*

We can then sum up the differences between the two experiences of receiving the Holy Spirit associated respectively with Resurrection Sunday and Pentecost Sunday.

On Resurrection Sunday it was:
>> the resurrected Christ
>> the inbreathed Spirit
>> the result: life.

On Pentecost Sunday it was:
>> the ascended Christ
>> the outpoured Spirit
>> the result: power.

The experience of the apostles demonstrates that salvation, or the new birth, and the baptism in the Holy Spirit are two distinct and separate experiences. The apostles received the first of these experiences on Resurrection Sunday; the second, seven weeks later on Pentecost Sunday.

Further study in the book of Acts discloses that the two experiences are normally separate. Furthermore, from Pentecost Sunday onwards, the term to 'receive the Hoy Spirit' is applied always and only to the second experience - the baptism in the Holy Spirit. It is never again used to describe the new birth.

Further Outpourings Of The Spirit

There are three other occasions, subsequent to Pentecost, where Scripture describes what took place when people were baptised in the Holy Spirit. These were in Samaria, in Ephesus, and in the household of Cornelius. We will examine each of these in turn.

The ministry of Philip in Samaria is introduced in **Acts 8:5:**

> *Then Philip went down to the city of Samaria and preached Christ to them.*

In **Acts 8:12** the record continues:

> *But when they believed Philip as he preached the things concerning the kingdom of God and the name of Jesus Christ, both men and women were baptised.*

These people had now heard the truth of Christ preached to them by Philip; they had believed; they had been baptised. It would be unreasonable and unscriptural to deny that these people were saved.

In **Mark 16:15-16,** Christ commissions His apostles to preach the gospel:

> *And He said to them, "Go into all the world and preach the gospel to every creature.*
> *"He who believes and is baptised will be saved; but he who does not believe will be condemned."*

The people of Samaria had heard the gospel preached; they had believed and they had been baptised. Therefore we know, on the authority of Christ's own words, that they were saved. Yet these same people up to this time had not received the Holy Spirit. This is made clear as we read on further in **Acts 8:14-17:**

> *Now when the apostles who were at Jerusalem heard that Samaria had received the Word of God, they sent Peter and John to them,*
> *who, when they had come down, prayed for them that they might receive the Holy Spirit.*
> *For as yet He had fallen upon none of them. They had only been baptised in the name of the Lord Jesus.*
> *Then they laid hands on them, and they received the Holy Spirit.*

We see that the people of Samaria received salvation through the ministry of Philip; they received the Holy Spirit through the ministry of Peter and John. Their receiving the Holy Spirit was a separate experience, subsequent to their receiving salvation. Here, then, is a second scriptural example which indicates that it is possible for people to have been converted and to have become genuine Christians, but not yet to have received the Holy Spirit in the sense in which this phrase is used from Pentecost onwards.

In this connection is it interesting to notice that, in the passage in Acts chapter 8, we find two different forms of speech used. One speaks of 'receiving the Holy Spirit'; the other speaks of 'the Holy Spirit falling upon them.' However, the context makes it plain that these are not two different experiences, but two different aspects of one and the same experience.

Let us turn on to **Acts 19:1-6,** which describes how Paul came to Ephesus and met there certain people who are described as 'disciples.' The first question that Paul asked these people was:

"Did you receive the Holy Spirit when you believed?"

It is plain that Paul had been given the impression that these people were disciples of Christ. Obviously, if they were not Christians at all, there could have been no question of their having received the Holy Spirit, since this is received only through faith in Christ. However, by further questioning, Paul discovered that these people were not disciples of Christ at all, but only of John the Baptist, and so he then went on to preach to them the full gospel of Christ.

One fact emerges clearly from this incident so far. Obviously, if people always received the Holy Spirit automatically, as an immediate consequence of believing in Christ, it would be illogical and foolish for Paul to ask the question: *"Did you receive the Holy Spirit when you believed?"* The mere fact that Paul asked this question makes it clear that he recognised the possibility of people having become disciples, or believers in Christ, without having received the Holy Spirit.

This is confirmed by the record of events which follows in the next few verses. After Paul had explained the gospel of Christ to these people, we read, in **Acts 19:5:**

When they heard this, they were baptised in the name of the Lord Jesus.

These people had now heard and believed the gospel, and they had been baptised. As we have already shown in connection with the people of Samaria, on the authority of Christ's own words, people who have fulfilled the two conditions of believing and being baptised are thereby saved. Nevertheless, these people in Ephesus, just like those in Samaria, had not yet received the Holy Spirit. In Ephesus, just as in Samaria, this came as a separate and subsequent experience; and it is described in the next verse - **Acts 19:6:**

And when Paul had laid hands on them, the Holy Spirit came upon them, and they spoke with tongues and prophesied.

Here then, in the case of these people at Ephesus, is a third scriptural example which indicates that it is possible for people to have been converted, and to have become genuine Christians, but not yet to have received the Holy Spirit.

This conclusion drawn from the record of the book of Acts is further confirmed by what Paul says in his Epistle to the Ephesians. We must bear in mind that this group of disciples to whom Paul ministered in Ephesus were among the Ephesian Christians to whom he later wrote his epistle.

In **Ephesians 1:13,** Paul reminds these people of the successive stages in which they were originally converted and received the Holy Spirit. Speaking of their coming to believe in Christ, he says:

In whom you also trusted, after you heard the word of truth, the gospel of your salvation; in whom also, having believed, you were sealed with the Holy Spirit of promise.

Here Paul indicates that there were three separate, successive stages in their experience: first, they heard the gospel; second, they trusted, or believed, in Christ; third, they were sealed with the Holy Spirit. This agrees exactly with the historical record in **Acts 19,** which states that these people first heard the gospel; then they believed, and were baptised; finally, when Paul laid his hands upon them, the Holy Spirit came on them.

In both accounts alike - in Acts and in Ephesians - it

is absolutely clear that these people received the Holy Spirit, not simultaneously with conversion, but as a separate and subsequent experience, after conversion.

For a fourth example, of a different kind, we shall now briefly consider **Acts 10:34-48**. This passage records the sermon which Peter preached in the house of Cornelius, and the results which followed his preaching.

The Scripture here seems to indicate that as soon as Cornelius and his household heard the gospel and put their faith in Christ, they immediately received the Holy Spirit and spoke with tongues. However, we must add that, although in this instance these two experiences happened together, they still remain two quite distinct experiences.

Furthermore, the evidence that Cornelius and his household had received the Holy Spirit, was not the fact that they had put their faith in Christ, but the fact that, under the impulse of the Holy Spirit, they spoke with tongues.

In the account of what happened in the household of Cornelius, the following three different phrases are all used to describe the same experience: 'the Holy Spirit fell upon' them; 'the gift of the Holy Spirit had been poured out on' them; they 'received the Holy Spirit.' Again, in **Acts 11:15-17**, where Peter describes the same incident, he uses the following three phrases: 'the Holy Spirit fell upon them'; they were 'baptised with (in) the Holy Spirit'; 'God gave them the same gift' (of the Holy Spirit).

Earlier, in **Acts 8:15-17**, two similar phrases were used concerning the Samaritans: the Holy Spirit 'had fallen upon none of them'; 'they received the Holy Spirit.'

Putting these passages together, we find that, in all, a total of five different phrases are used to describe this one experience: 'the Holy Spirit fell upon them'; 'the gift of the Holy Spirit had been poured out on' them; they 'received the Holy Spirit'; they were 'baptised with (in) the Holy Spirit'; 'God gave them the gift' of the Holy Spirit.

Some modern interpreters would suggest that these different phrases refer to various different experiences. However, this is definitely not in line with the usage of the apostles in the New Testament. According to the apostles, these different phrases all denote one single experience -

although they describe it from different aspects.

It is the same thing for a person to receive the Holy Spirit, or to receive the gift of the Holy Spirit, as it is for that person to be baptised in the Holy Spirit, or for the Holy Spirit to fall upon that person, or for the Holy Spirit to be poured out on that person.

We have now carefully considered, in all, four different groups of people portrayed in the New Testament; first, the apostles; second, the people of Samaria; third, the disciples at Ephesus; fourth, Cornelius and his household. Of these four groups, we have seen clearly that the first three - the apostles, the people of Samaria, the disciples at Ephesus - had all been converted and become Christians, **before** they received the Holy Spirit. Their receiving the Holy Spirit was a separate and subsequent experience, following their conversion.

A careful examination of the whole of the rest of the New Testament would seem to show that there is no other instance recorded, apart from Cornelius and his household, in which people received the Holy Spirit at the same time as they believed in Christ. We are therefore justified in concluding that, in this respect, the experience of Cornelius and his household is the exception, rather than the rule.

On the basis of this careful examination of the New Testament record, we may now set forth the following conclusions.

First, it is normal for a Christian to receive the Holy Spirit as a separate and subsequent experience, following conversion.

Second, even if a person receives the Holy Spirit at the same time as conversion, receiving the Holy Spirit still remains, logically, a quite distinct experience from being converted.

Third, whether a person receives the Holy Spirit at the same time as conversion, or following after conversion, the evidence that that person has received the Holy Spirit still remains the same: the person speaks with tongues, as the Holy Spirit gives utterance.

Fourth, as a logical consequence of the foregoing - the fact that a person has been genuinely converted and has become a real Christian, does not by itself constitute evidence that that person has received the Holy Spirit.

The Teaching Of Jesus

This conclusion concerning the relationship between conversion and receiving the Holy Spirit has been based mainly on a study of the book of Acts. However, it is in full accord with the teaching of Jesus Himself on this same topic in the Gospels.

For example, in **Luke 11:13,** Jesus says to His disciples:

"If you then, being evil, know how to give good gifts to your children, how much more will your heavenly Father give the Holy Spirit to those who ask Him!"

The teaching of this verse - reinforced by the examples, which precede it, of a son asking his father successively for bread, for a fish, and for an egg - is clearly to the effect that God, as a heavenly Father, is willing to give the Holy Spirit to His believing children, if they will ask for it. However, a person must first be converted and put his faith in Christ, in order to become a child of God.

Plainly, therefore, Jesus teaches not that the Holy Spirit is received at conversion, but rather that it is a gift which every converted believer thereafter has a right to ask for, as a child from its Father. Furthermore, Jesus here definitely places an obligation upon the children of God to ask their heavenly Father specifically for this gift of the Holy Spirit. It is therefore not scriptural for a Christian to assume, or to assert, that he automatically received the gift of the Holy Spirit at conversion, without asking for it.

Again, in **John 7:38,** Christ says:

"He who believes in Me, as the Scripture has said, out of his heart will flow rivers of living water."

In the first half of the next verse these *rivers of living water* are interpreted by the writer of the Gospel as referring to the Holy Spirit, for he says:

But this He spoke concerning the Spirit, whom those believing in Him would receive...

In both these verses it is made plain that the gift of the Holy

Spirit, bringing forth rivers of living water from within, is to be received by those who are already believers in Christ. It is something which they should go on to receive, after believing in Christ.

Christ teaches the same truth again in **John 14:15-17,** where He says:

"If you love Me, keep My commandments.
And I will pray the Father, and He will give you another Helper, that he may abide with you forever, even the Spirit of truth, whom the world cannot receive, because it neither sees Him nor knows Him; but you know Him, for He dwells with you and will be in you."

In this passage, the *Helper* and *the Spirit of truth* are two different designations of the Holy Spirit. Christ teaches here plainly that the gift of the Holy Spirit is not for the unbelieving people of this world, but for Christ's own disciples who love and obey Him. This confirms therefore that it is the privilege of God's believing children, Christ's disciples, to go on to receive the gift of the Holy Spirit, as they meet God's conditions. These may be summed up in one all-important requirement: loving obedience to Christ.

Chapter 7

DO ALL SPEAK WITH TONGUES?

We shall now go on to consider some other objections, or misunderstandings, which commonly arise in connection with the experience of speaking in tongues.

The Gift Of 'Kinds Of Tongues'

One common objection, or misunderstanding, is based on the words of the apostle Paul in **1 Corinthians 12:30,** where he asks: *'Do all speak with tongues?'* A careful examination of the context shows that Paul clearly implies that the answer to his question is 'No - all do not speak with tongues.'

Does this mean, then, that there were Christians in the New Testament church who had received the baptism in the Holy Spirit without speaking with tongues?

No, this is not what Paul is saying. Paul is not here speaking about the baptism in the Holy Spirit, but about various possible ministries, or supernatural manifestations, of the Spirit, which can be exercised by the believer in the church, subsequent to, and as a result of, the initial experience of being baptised in the Holy Spirit.

This agrees with what Paul says two verses previously, in **1 Corinthians 12:27-28:**

> Now you are the body of Christ, and members individually.
> And God has appointed these in the church: first apostles, second prophets, third teachers, after that miracles, then gifts of healings, helps, administrations, varieties of tongues.

71

Paul is here speaking of various different ministries which may be exercised by different members within the church. Amongst these he enumerates *varieties of tongues* or - more literally - 'kinds of tongues.'

Exactly the same expression is used by Paul still earlier in the same chapter. In **1 Corinthians 12:7-11**, Paul enumerates nine different possible gifts, or manifestations, of the Holy Spirit, which may be granted to believers who have been baptised in the Holy Spirit. The list is as follows:

> But the manifestation of the Spirit is given to each one for the profit of all:
> for to one is given the word of wisdom through the Spirit, to another the word of knowledge through the same Spirit,
> to another faith by the same Spirit, to another gifts of healing by the same Spirit,
> to another the working of miracles, to another prophecy,
> to another discerning of spirits, to another different kinds of tongues, to another interpretation of tongues.
> But one and the same Spirit works all of these things, distributing to each one individually as He wills.

Paul is here speaking about manifestations or gifts of the Spirit that may be exercised by believers subsequent to their receiving the initial baptism in the Spirit. This is confirmed by what he says two verses further on in **1 Corinthians 12:13**:

> For by one Spirit we were all baptised into one body...

Or, more literally, and more clearly: '*For in one Spirit we were baptised into one body...*'

Paul here speaks of the baptism in the Spirit as an experience that has already been received by those to whom he writes. The nine gifts, or manifestations, of the Spirit, which he lists, may then be exercised by believers subsequent to, and as a result of, their having initially been baptised in the Holy Spirit.

Paul indicates that though the initial baptism in the Holy Spirit is for all believers - *in one Spirit we were all baptised into one body* - thereafter the various gifts, or manifestations, of the Spirit are divided up amongst the believers according to the sovereign will of the Spirit Himself. One believer may receive one gift, and another believer may receive another gift. Not all believers receive all the gifts.

Among the nine gifts of the Spirit listed by Paul, the eighth is *different kinds of tongues.* The phrase in the original Greek - *kinds of tongues* - is exactly the same as that translated 'varieties of tongues' in **1 Corinthians 12:28.** In each case, Paul is speaking about a specific spiritual gift, not about the initial baptism in the Holy Spirit.

It is outside the scope of our present study to examine the exact operation of this particular gift. It is sufficient for our present purposes to have established the fact that in **1 Corinthians 12:28** - as in verse **10** of the same chapter - Paul is not talking about the initial experience of being baptised in the Holy Spirit, but about one of the nine spiritual gifts exercised by some believers (but not by all) as a result of the baptism in the Holy Spirit.

From this it follows that, in **1 Corinthians 12:30,** when Paul says *'Do all speak with tongues?',* the question which he has in mind is not: 'Have all at one time spoken in tongues?' - that is, when they were initially baptised in the Holy Spirit. On the contrary, the question with which he is now concerned is this: 'Do all believers, who have been baptised in the Holy Spirit, thereafter regularly exercise the gift of kinds of tongues?' To this question the answer - both then, and now - is a definite 'No.' In this respect, the experience of modern believers after being baptised in the Spirit is in full accord with the pattern established in the New Testament.

This distinction between the initial gift of the Holy Spirit Himself, attested by the evidence of speaking in tongues, and the subsequent gift of *kinds of tongues,* is very carefully preserved by the linguistic usage of the New Testament. The Greek word used in the New Testament for 'gift,' when it denotes the gift of the Holy Spirit Himself, received at the baptism in the Spirit, is *dorea.* The Greek word for 'gift,' when it denotes any of the nine different gifts, or manifestations, of the Spirit (including the gift of 'kinds of tongues') is *charisma.*

These two words are never interchanged in the New

Testament. *Charisma* is never used to denote the gift of the Holy Spirit Himself, initially received at the baptism in the Spirit. Conversely, *dorea* is never used to denote any of the nine separate and subsequent gifts of the Holy Spirit, manifested in the lives of the believers who have already received the baptism in the Holy Spirit. The language, the teaching, and the examples of the New Testament all alike indicate a clear distinction between these two aspects of spiritual experience.

Is Fruit The Evidence?

Those who claim that speaking with tongues is not necessarily the evidence of having received the baptism in the Holy Spirit are obliged by logic to suggest some alternative form of evidence by which we may know, according to Scripture, that a person has received the baptism in the Holy Spirit.

One such form of alternative evidence which is quite commonly proposed is that of spiritual fruit. The suggestion is that unless a person demonstrates in his life the fruit of the Holy Spirit in a very clear and full way, then that person cannot be considered to have received the baptism in the Holy Spirit.

The complete list of the fruit of the Holy Spirit is given by Paul in **Galatians 5:22-23:**

> But the fruit of the Spirit is love, joy, peace, long-suffering, kindness, goodness, faithfulness, gentleness, self-control.

This, and other passages, make it plain that the primary form of the fruit of the Spirit, out of which all the rest develop, is *love.*

Now only a very foolish and shallow-minded Christian would ever deny that spiritual fruit in general, and love in particular, are of supreme importance in the life of every Christian. This does not mean, however, that spiritual fruit can be accepted as the scriptural evidence of having received the baptism in the Holy Spirit. In fact, this test of spiritual fruit must be rejected as being contrary to Scripture on two main grounds: first, it is not the test which the apostles

74

themselves applied; second, it overlooks the clear, scriptural distinction between a gift and fruit.

Let us consider first the test which the apostles applied in their own experience. When the 120 disciples on the day of Pentecost received the baptism in the Holy Spirit, with the outward evidence of speaking with other tongues, the apostle Peter did not wait several weeks or months to see whether this experience would produce in the lives of himself and the other disciples a much greater measure of spiritual fruit than they had previously enjoyed. On the contrary, he stood up the very same hour, and said without any doubts or qualifications:

> *"But this is what was spoken by the prophet Joel:*
> *'And it shall come to pass in the last days, says God,*
> *That I will pour out of My Spirit on all flesh…'"*

What evidence did Peter have for making this statement? Nothing but the fact that they all began to speak with other tongues. No further evidence besides this was required.

Again, in **Acts 8,** we read that after many people in Samaria had been converted through the preaching of Philip, the apostles Peter and John then went down to pray for them that they might receive the Holy Spirit. The record of what took place is given in **Acts 8:14-20:**

> *Now when the apostles who were at Jerusalem heard that Samaria had received the Word of God, they sent Peter and John to them,*
> *who, when they had come down, prayed for them that they might receive the Holy Spirit.*
> *For as yet He had fallen upon none of them. They had only been baptised in the name of the Lord Jesus.*
> *Then they laid hands on them, and they received the Holy Spirit.*
> *Now when Simon saw that through the laying on of the apostles' hands the Holy Spirit was given, he offered them money,*
> *saying, "Give me this power also, that anyone on whom I lay hands may receive the Holy Spirit."*

But Peter said to him, "Your money perish with you, because you thought that the gift of God could be purchased with money!"

From this account we understand that these people in Samaria had only been converted for a matter of a few days, or at the most a few weeks. Yet they received the Holy Spirit through the laying on of the apostles' hands as a single, complete experience.

Thereafter there was no question of waiting to see whether in the course of the ensuing weeks and months sufficient spiritual fruit would be manifested in the lives of these new converts to prove that they really had received the Holy Spirit. No, their receiving the Holy Spirit was a single, complete experience, after which no further evidence or tests were needed.

The objection is sometimes raised that the Scripture does not explicitly state that these people in Samaria spoke with tongues when they received the Holy Spirit. This is quite true. However, the Scripture does make it plain that, through the laying on of the apostles' hands, there was an open demonstration of supernatural power such that Simon, who had been a professional sorcerer, was willing to pay money in order that he might receive the power to produce a similar supernatural demonstration in any people upon whom he in turn might thereafter lay his hands.

If we accept that these people in Samaria, as a result of the laying on of the apostles' hands, spoke with other tongues as the Holy Spirit gave them utterance, this will fit in with every detail of the story as it is recorded in the book of Acts, and it will also bring their experience into line with the cases of all the other people in the book of Acts who are known to have received the baptism in the Holy Spirit.

On the other hand, if people prefer to assume that in this particular incident in Samaria there was some other supernatural manifestation, which was not speaking with tongues, they must at least acknowledge that we have no way whatever of finding out what form this other kind of manifestation may have taken.

Upon this assumption, therefore, it is not possible to build any kind of positive doctrinal conclusion concerning the baptism in the Holy Spirit. For example, a person cannot say: 'I have not spoken with tongues; nevertheless I know that I have received the baptism in the Holy Spirit because I have received the same evidence, or experience, as the people of Samaria.' If the people of Samaria did not speak with tongues there is no way of knowing what else they may have done instead.

Thus, this assumption that the people of Samaria did not speak with tongues leads only to conclusions which are completely negative and sterile. It cannot in any way affect the positive conclusions which we have been able to form from the other cases where we know that people, on receiving the baptism in the Spirit, did speak with tongues.

Another case which is sometimes brought forward in this connection is that of Saul of Tarsus - later the apostle Paul. The climax of Paul's conversion, and the events which accompanied it, is related in **Acts 9:17-18:**

And Ananias went his way and entered the house; and laying his hands on him he said, "Brother Saul, the Lord Jesus, who appeared to you on the road as you came, has sent me that you may receive your sight and be filled with the Holy Spirit."
Immediately there fell from his eyes something like scales, and he received his sight at once; and he arose and was baptised.

Surely if there was ever a case where the early church might justifiably have applied the test of fruit, it was in the case of Saul of Tarsus, now about to become Paul. Up to that time Paul had been, on his own admission, the bitterest opponent of the gospel and persecutor of the church. Yet here we find him receiving the Holy Spirit, in a single experience, through the laying on of the hands of Ananias, and thereafter there is not the faintest suggestion that any further test of fruit in his life might have to be applied.

Once again, in this case of Paul, there are those who object that the Scripture does not state that Paul spoke with tongues when Ananias laid hands on him. It is true that the Scripture here gives no details whatever of what happened to Paul. However, side by side with this account in **Acts 9,** we must set Paul's own personal testimony in **1 Corinthians 14:18,** where he says:

> *I thank my God I speak with tongues more than you all...*

When we combine this testimony of Paul's with the other examples given in the book of Acts, it becomes only natural and reasonable to conclude that Paul first began to speak with tongues when Ananias laid his hands upon him that he might be filled with the Spirit. This conclusion is further strengthened by the subsequent record of **Acts 19:6,** which describes what happened when Paul in turn laid hands on new believers at Ephesus:

> *And when Paul had laid hands on them, the Holy Spirit came upon them, and they spoke with tongues and prophesied.*

It would be unnatural to suppose that Paul laid his hands upon these converts in order to transmit to them an experience which he had never received himself.

One further, and decisive, case is that of Cornelius and his household, as related in **Acts 10.** Peter and the other believing Jews went to the house of Cornelius with reluctance, against their own inclinations, only because God had explicitly directed them to go. After Peter had been preaching a short while, the Holy Spirit fell upon all who heard his word. Peter and the other Jews were amazed, because they heard these Gentiles speaking with tongues.

Up to this very moment Peter, like other Jewish believers, had not conceived that it was possible for Gentiles, such as Cornelius, to be saved and become Christians. Yet this one manifestation of speaking with tongues immediately convinced Peter and the other Jews that these Gentiles were now just as much Christians as the Jews themselves. Peter never suggested that it would be necessary to subject these Gentiles to any further tests, or to wait for spiritual fruit, or look for any other kind of evidence. On the contrary, he immediately commanded that they be baptised, by which act they were openly accepted and attested as full Christians.

In **Acts 11:15** and **17,** Peter gives an account of this incident to the other leaders of the apostolic church in Jerusalem:

> *"And as I began to speak, the Holy Spirit fell upon them, as upon us at the beginning...*
> *"If therefore God gave them the same gift as He gave us when we believed on the Lord Jesus Christ, who was I that I could withstand God?"*

We know from the previous chapter that Cornelius and his household all spoke with tongues. Yet in this account Peter does not find it necessary to mention this decisive manifestation. He merely says: *"the Holy Spirit fell upon them, as upon us at the beginning...God gave them the same gift as He gave us..."* In other words, the manifestation of speaking with tongues was at this time so universally accepted as the evidence of receiving the Holy Spirit, that Peter did not even need to mention it. Both he, and the other church leaders, took it for granted.

The conclusion of the other church leaders is stated in the next verse - **Acts 11:18:**

> *When they heard these things they became silent; and they glorified God, saying, "Then God has also granted to the Gentiles repentance to life."*

What convinced Peter and the other apostles that Gentiles could experience salvation through faith in Christ just as fully as Jews? One thing, and one thing only: the fact that they heard these Gentiles speak with tongues. In the whole of this account there is never any suggestion that Peter or any other of the apostles ever looked for any other kind of evidence in these Gentiles' lives, apart from the fact that they spoke with tongues. There was no question of waiting for spiritual fruit to be manifested.

In this, the apostles were perfectly logical. Not because fruit is unimportant, but because fruit is, by its very nature, totally different from a gift. A gift is received by a single act of faith; fruit is produced by a slow, gradual process, which includes planting, tending, and cultivating.

The baptism in the Holy Spirit is a gift - a single experience - received by faith. The evidence that a person has received this gift is that he speaks with other tongues.

Thereafter, one main purpose for which the gift is given is to enable the person to produce more and better spiritual fruit than he could ever otherwise have produced. It is no error to emphasise the importance of fruit. The error consists in confusing a gift with a fruit, in confusing the evidence that a gift has been received with the purpose for which the gift has been given.

In the next chapter we shall go on to consider a number of other common misunderstandings connected with tongues as the evidence of having received the baptism in the Holy Spirit.

Chapter 8

EMOTIONAL AND PHYSICAL REACTIONS

One view which is commonly held today is that the baptism in the Holy Spirit is, first and foremost, an intense emotional experience. One word with strong emotional associations quite often used in this connection is the word 'ecstasy.' This view of the baptism in the Holy Spirit would seem to draw its support mainly from two sources.

First, there are some theologians, who do not actually have the experience themselves, but who theorise about it on the basis of passages in the New Testament or in the writings of the early Church Fathers. For some reason or other, these theologians seem to have chosen the word 'ecstasy,' or 'ecstatic,' as a good theological sounding word, with which to sum up the essential nature of this supernatural experience.

Second, there are many believers who have actually received the experience, and who, by a common tendency of human nature, when testifying of it to others, lay the main emphasis on their own subjective, emotional reactions. The result is that they convey to those who hear them, often without meaning to do so, the impression that the essential nature of the experience is emotional. Probably the particular emotion most commonly mentioned in this connection is that of 'joy.'

The Place Of Emotion

Now, in considering the relationship between the emotions and the baptism in the Holy Spirit, we do well to begin by acknowledging two important facts.

First, man is an emotional creature. His emotions

constitute an integral and important part of his total make-up. Therefore, man's emotions have an important part to play in his total worship and service of God. True conversion neither suppresses nor obliterates a man's emotions. True conversion, on the contrary, first liberates, and then redirects, a man's emotions. If a man's emotions have not entered into his total experience of conversion - if they have not been brought under the control and the power of the Holy Spirit, then that man is not yet fully converted.

Second, we must also acknowledge that in Scripture, the word 'joy' is often closely associated with the Holy Spirit. For instance, the fruit of the Spirit, as listed in **Galatians 5:22,** is first 'love,' then 'joy,' and so on. In this list, 'joy' comes immediately after love itself, which is the primary form of the fruit of the Spirit. Again, we read, in **Acts 13:52,** concerning the early Christians in the city of Antioch:

And the disciples were filled with joy and with the Holy Spirit.

We see then that, in the New Testament, joy is often closely associated with the Holy Spirit.

Nevertheless, the teaching that intense joy, or any other strong emotion, by itself constitutes evidence of the baptism in the Holy Spirit, cannot be reconciled with the New Testament. For this, there are two main reasons.

First, in the actual passages where the baptism in the Holy Spirit is described, there is never any direct mention whatever of emotion. Never once is any form of emotion depicted either as the evidence, or as the direct consequence, of having received the Holy Spirit.

Any person who equates receiving the Holy Spirit with an emotional experience has no scriptural basis for his doctrine. This is quite contrary to the thinking of the natural man, and usually surprises the average religious person who does not base his opinions directly on the New Testament.

In fact, it sometimes happens that believers, seeking the Holy Spirit, receive a clear, scriptural experience of speaking with other tongues exactly as recorded in the New Testament; and yet they are afterwards unconvinced and dissatisfied with their experience, simply because they were not conscious of any intense or wonderful emotion, such as they had wrongly been led to expect.

We may illustrate this by the example of a little boy who asks his parents for a spaniel puppy as a birthday present. When the present arrives, it is a beautiful golden cocker spaniel puppy, exhibiting all the marks of a real pedigree spaniel of its class.

Nevertheless, to the parents' dismay, the little boy who receives this gift is obviously far from satisfied with it. When his parents seek the reason for his dissatisfaction, they discover that all the little fellow's friends have been telling him for weeks past that all spaniels are black, and therefore he has formed in advance a strong expectation that the puppy which he is to receive will be black.

No matter how beautiful the golden puppy may be, it cannot now satisfy him, simply because it fails to live up to his expectation of being black. Yet his opinion that all spaniels are black has no basis at all in fact, but has been formed merely by listening to the opinions of friends his own age, who know no more about spaniels than he himself.

So it is sometimes with Christians who ask their heavenly Father for the gift of the Holy Spirit. In answer to their prayer they receive an experience of speaking with other tongues which is in perfect accord with the examples and the teaching of the New Testament.

Yet they are not satisfied with this scriptural answer to their prayers, simply because it did not happen to be marked by any intense emotional experience. They fail to realise that their anticipation of some intense emotion was based in the first instance on the ill-considered opinions of misguided fellow Christians, not on the clear teaching of the New Testament.

The second reason why we cannot accept any strong emotion, like joy, as evidence of receiving the Holy Spirit is that there are instances in the New Testament of believers who experienced a wonderful sense of joy, but who nevertheless had not yet received the Holy Spirit. For instance, we read in **Luke 24:52-53,** concerning the first disciples, after the ascension of Jesus, but before the day of Pentecost:

*And they worshiped Him and returned to Jerusalem
with great joy,
and were continually in the temple praising and blessing
God.*

Here we find that the disciples, even before the day of
Pentecost, experienced great joy in their worship of God.
Nevertheless, we know that it was not until the day of
Pentecost itself that they were actually baptised in the Holy
Spirit.

Again, we read in **Acts 8:8,** the following description
of the city of Samaria, after the people of the city had heard
and believed the gospel of Christ, preached to them by
Philip: *And there was great joy in that city.*

We see that the whole-hearted acceptance of the gospel
immediately brought great joy to these Samaritans. Nevertheless, as we read on in the same chapter, we discover that
it was only later, through the ministry of Peter and John,
that these people received the Holy Spirit.

These two examples of the first disciples, and of the
people of Samaria, prove, therefore, that an intense
emotional experience, such as great joy, is not an essential
part of the baptism in the Holy Spirit, and cannot be
accepted as evidence of having received this baptism.

Physical Reactions

Another type of experience often associated by some
people with the baptism in the Holy Spirit is some kind of
very powerful physical sensation in their body. Over the
course of years I have had occasion to question many people
as to the grounds on which they based their claim to have
received the baptism in the Holy Spirit, and I have found
that people often associate this experience with some very
strong physical sensation, or reaction.

The following are some of the experiences which have
actually been mentioned to me, in this connection, at various
times: a sensation as of a very powerful electric current; a
sensation as of a fire, or of intense heat in some other form;
being prostrated forcefully on the floor; a powerful shak-
ing of the whole body; seeing a very bright light; hearing

the actual voice of God speaking; having a vision of heavenly glories; and so on.

Once again, in considering theories of this kind, we must acknowledge that they contain an important element of truth. Throughout the course of the Bible we find many instances where the immediate presence and power of almighty God produced strong physical reactions in the bodies of those of His people who were counted worthy to come close to Him.

In **Genesis 17:1-3,** we read that when the Lord appeared to Abraham and began to speak to him, Abraham fell upon his face. Several times in the books of Leviticus and Numbers, when God's presence and glory were visibly manifested among His people, both Moses and Aaron and others also of the children of Israel fell upon their faces. In **1 Kings 18:39,** when the fire fell upon Elijah's sacrifice and all the people saw it, they fell upon their faces. In **2 Chronicles 5:13-14,** we read, concerning the dedication of Solomon's temple:

> ...*the house of the Lord, was filled with a cloud,*
> *so that the priests could not continue ministering* (more literally, could not stand to minister) *because of the cloud; for the glory of the Lord filled the house of God.*

There are two passages in which the prophet Jeremiah gives his own personal testimony of the strong physical effects produced within him by the power of God's Word and God's presence.

In **Jeremiah 20:9,** he says:

> *Then I said, "I will not make mention of Him* (that is, of the Lord),
> *Nor speak anymore in His name."*
> *But His word was in my heart like a burning fire*
> *Shut up in my bones;*
> *I was weary of holding it back,*
> *And I could not.*

Here Jeremiah testifies that the prophetic message of the Lord within his heart produced the impression of a burning fire in his bones.

A little further on, in **Jeremiah 23:9,** he says again:

My heart within me is broken
Because of the prophets;
All my bones shake.
I am like a drunken man whom wine has overcome,
Because of the Lord, (more literally, from the face,
or presence of the Lord)
And because of His Holy words.

Here also, Jeremiah's words indicate a most powerful physical reaction to God's presence.

Again, in **Daniel 10:7-8,** we read of the powerful physical effects produced upon Daniel and his companions by a direct vision of the Lord.

And I, Daniel, alone saw the vision, for the men who were with me did not see the vision; but a great terror (or trembling) *fell upon them, so that they fled to hide themselves.*
Therefore I was left alone when I saw this great vision, and no strength remained in me; for my vigour was turned to frailty in me, and I retained no strength.

At the immediate presence of the Lord, Daniel and his companions - just like Jeremiah - experienced strong and unusual physical reactions.

Nor are reactions of this kind confined to the Old Testament. In **Acts 9:3-6,** we read of the vision of the Lord granted to Saul of Tarsus on his way to Damascus. Saul saw a very bright light; he heard a voice speaking to him from heaven; he fell to the earth; and his body trembled.

Again, in **Revelation 1:10-17,** John describes a vision of the Lord he received on the island of Patmos, and he concludes:

And when I saw Him, I fell at His feet as dead...

Here, too, there was obviously a very powerful and dramatic physical reaction to the immediate presence of the Lord.

In some of the older denominations of the Christian church there is a tendency to dismiss all such physical reactions or manifestations as these, with labels such as 'emotionalism,' or 'fanaticism.' However, this attitude plainly goes far beyond what Scripture warrants.

Doubtless, there can be occasions when manifestations of this kind are the product of 'emotionalism,' or 'fanaticism,' or possibly of a carnal desire for self-display. But who would dare to bring charges such as these against men like the prophets Moses, Jeremiah and Daniel, or the apostles John and Paul? Too often the tendency to reject all forms of physical reaction to the presence and power of God is based on false, man-made traditions of what constitutes true holiness, or of the kind or behaviour that is acceptable to God in the worship of His people.

We see then, that the Scripture gives room for various forms of powerful, or unusual, reactions in the bodies of God's people, caused by special experiences of His immediate presence, or power. However, nowhere is it ever suggested that any of these physical reactions or manifestations, constitute evidence that a person has received the baptism in the Holy Spirit.

In the cases of the Old Testament prophets, such as Moses, or Jeremiah, or Daniel, we know that none of these received the baptism in the Holy Spirit, because this experience was never granted to anyone before the day of Pentecost. In the cases of John and Paul in the New Testament, it is equally clear that the strong physical reactions which they experienced to the presence of the Lord were not evidence of their receiving the baptism in the Spirit.

At the time when John received his vision on Patmos, he had already been baptised in the Spirit for more than fifty years. On the other hand, Paul's physical reactions on the Damascus road happened before he was filled with the Holy Spirit. He received this infilling as a separate, subsequent experience three days later, when Ananias laid hands on him in Damascus.

No matter from what angle we may approach this subject, we are always brought to the same conclusion: there is one, and only one, physical manifestation which constitutes evidence that a person has received the Holy Spirit. That manifestation is speaking with other tongues, as the Spirit gives utterance.

Three Scriptural Principles

In closing this study, let us consider briefly three different, but basic, principles of Scripture, all of which confirm that speaking with other tongues is the appropriate evidence that a person has received the Holy Spirit.

First in **Matthew 12:34,** Jesus says:.

"...For out of the abundance of the heart the mouth speaks."

In other words, the heart of man, when it is filled to overflowing, overflows in speech through the mouth. This applies to the baptism in the Holy Spirit. When a person's heart has been filled to overflowing with the Holy Spirit, the overflow of the heart then takes place in speech through the mouth. Because the infilling is supernatural, the overflow is supernatural also. The person speaks a language which he has never learned and does not understand, using this to glorify God.

Second, in **Romans 6:13,** Paul exhorts us as Christians:

...present yourselves to God as being alive from the dead, and your members as instruments of righteousness to God.

God's requirements go beyond the mere surrender of ourselves - that is, our wills - to Him. He demands that we actually present to Him our physical members, that He may control them according to His own will as instruments of righteousness.

However, in **James 3:8,** we are reminded that there is one member of the body which none of us can control:

But no man can tame (or control) *the tongue. It is an unruly evil, full of deadly poison.*

As the final evidence, or seal, that the presenting of our physical members to God has been made complete, the Spirit of God takes control of the very member which none of us can control - that is, the tongue - and then uses this member in a supernatural way for God's glory.

The third principle of Scripture that establishes the relationship between tongues and the baptism in the Spirit is derived from the very nature of the Holy Spirit Himself.

In various passages, Jesus is careful to emphasise that the Spirit is a real Person - just as real as God the Father and God the Son. For instance, in **John 16:13,** Jesus says:

"However, when He, the Spirit of truth, has come, He will guide you into all truth; for He will not speak on His own authority, but whatever He hears He will speak..."

Here Jesus emphasises the personality of the Holy Spirit in two ways: first, by using the pronoun 'He' (rather than 'it'); second, by attributing to the Holy Spirit the ability to speak. Reflection will show that the ability to speak is one of the decisive, distinguishing features of personality. To anything capable of speaking for itself we naturally attribute the concept of a person; but if anything lacks this ability to speak, we should not normally consider it a person. The fact that the Holy Spirit speaks directly for Himself is one of the great marks of His true personality.

Side by side with this we may set the words of Paul in **1 Corinthians 6:19:**

Or do you not know that your body is the temple of the Holy Spirit who is in you...

Here Paul teaches that the physical body of the redeemed believer is the appointed temple in which the Holy Spirit desires to dwell. Appropriately therefore, the evidence that the Holy Spirit, as a Person, has come to take up His dwelling in this physical temple is that He exercises the attribute of personality and speaks from within the temple, using the tongue and the lips of the believer himself to make this speech audible.

So it was also in the tabernacle of Moses. In **Numbers 7:89,** we read that when Moses went into the tabernacle to commune with God,

...he heard the voice of One speaking to him from above the mercy seat.

Because Moses heard this voice - the mark of personality - he knew that the Person of the Lord Himself was present in the tabernacle. In like manner today, when we hear the voice of the Holy Spirit speaking audibly from within the temple of a believer's body, we know, by this evidence of personality, that the Holy Spirit Himself - the Third Person of the Godhead - has taken up residence within the believer.

We find, then, that speaking with other tongues as the evidence of the baptism in the Holy Spirit, accords with three great principles of Scripture.

First, the heart of the believer, supernaturally filled with the Holy Spirit, overflows supernaturally in speech through his mouth.

Second, the evidence that the believer has yielded his physical members to God, is that God's Spirit controls that member - the tongue - which the believer cannot control for himself.

Third, by speaking from within the temple of the believer's body, the Holy Spirit demonstrates that He now dwells there as a Person.

Chapter 9

THE PROMISE OF THE SPIRIT

In the preceding four chapters we have carefully analysed the teaching of the New Testament concerning the baptism in the Holy Spirit. Our analysis has included the following topics: the nature of the experience; the outward evidence by which it is attested; how it differs from the gift of 'kinds of tongues'; the place of emotional and physical reactions.

This leads naturally to a practical question. What are the conditions which must be fulfilled before a person can receive this experience of being baptised in the Holy Spirit? There are two different possible ways to approach this question. The first is from the viewpoint of God, the giver of the gift; the second is from the viewpoint of man, the receiver. In this chapter we shall approach the question from the first viewpoint - that of God Himself. In the next chapter we shall approach it from the human viewpoint.

The question which now confronts us is awesome in its implications. On what basis can a holy and omnipotent God offer to members of a fallen, sin-cursed race the gift of His own Spirit to indwell their physical bodies? What provision could God make to bridge the measureless gulf separating man from Himself?

The answer is supplied by a plan of redemption which was conceived in the eternal council of the Godhead before time began. Central to the outworking of this whole plan was the sacrificial death of Christ on the cross, which was followed first by His victorious resurrection and then by His triumphant ascension. Ten days later He poured out the Holy Spirit on His waiting disciples. Viewed in this light, the cross is seen as the gate that opened the way to Pentecost.

A Personal Permanent Indwelling

The direct connection between the ascension of Jesus and the outpouring of the Holy Spirit at Pentecost is unfolded in **John 7:37-39:**

On the last day, that great day of the feast, Jesus stood and cried out, saying, "If anyone thirsts, let him come to Me and drink.

"He who believes in Me, as the Scripture has said, out of his heart will flow rivers of living water."

But this He spoke concerning the Spirit, whom those believing in Him would receive; for the Holy Spirit was not yet given, because Jesus was not yet glorified.

The first two verses in this passage contain the actual promise of Jesus Himself, that every thirsty soul, who comes to Him with scriptural faith, will be filled and become a channel for rivers of living water. The last verse of the passage is an explanation of the two previous verses, added by the writer of the Gospel.

In this explanation, the writer points out two things: first, the promise of the rivers of living water refers to the gift of the Holy Spirit; second, this gift could not be given while Jesus Himself was still on earth in bodily form. It could only be made available to believers after Jesus Himself had been received up to heaven again and had there entered into His glory, at the Father's right hand.

What precisely is meant by saying that the Holy Spirit could not be given at that time? Obviously this does not mean that the Holy Spirit could not in any way be present, or move and work in the earth, until after the ascension of Christ into heaven. On the contrary, as early as the second verse of the Bible - **Genesis 1:2** - we already read of the Holy Spirit at work in the world:

...And the Spirit of God was hovering over the face of the waters.

From this time onwards, throughout the whole of the Old Testament and on into the days of Christ's earthly ministry, we read continually of the Holy Spirit moving and working in many different ways in the world at large, and more particularly amongst the believing people of God. What then was the difference between the way in which the Holy Spirit worked up to the time of Christ's ascension into glory, and the gift of the Holy Spirit, which was reserved for Christian believers after Christ's ascension, and which was first received by the disciples in Jerusalem on the day of Pentecost?

There are three descriptive words which sum up the distinctive features of this gift of the Holy Spirit, and which thus distinguish it from all previous operations of the Holy Spirit in the world. These three words are: **personal; indwelling; permanent.** Let us briefly consider, in turn, the significance of each of these three features.

First the gift of the Holy Spirit is **personal.**

In **John 16:7,** in His farewell discourse to His disciples, Jesus indicated that there was to be an exchange of divine Persons:

> *"Nevertheless I tell you the truth. It is to your advantage that I go away; for if I do not go away, the Helper will not come to you; but if I depart, I will send Him to you."*

In effect, Jesus was saying: "In personal presence, I am about to leave you and return to heaven. In My place, however, I will send you another Person - the Holy Spirit. This will be to your advantage."

The promise of the coming of the Holy Spirit as a Person was fulfilled at Pentecost. Since then, the Holy Spirit seeks to come to each believer individually, as a Person. We can no longer speak merely of an influence, or an operation, or a manifestation, or of some impersonal power. The Holy Spirit is just as much a Person as God the Father, or God the Son; and it is in this individual and personal way that He now seeks, in this dispensation, to come to the believer.

In the experience of salvation, or the new birth, the sinner receives Christ, the Son of God, the Second Person of the Godhead. In the experience of the baptism in the Holy Spirit, the believer receives the Third Person of the Godhead, the Holy Spirit. In each experience alike, there is an absolutely real and direct transaction with a Person.

Second, the Holy Spirit in this dispensation comes to **indwell** the believer.

In the Old Testament the moving of the Holy Spirit amongst God's people is characteristically described by phrases such as these: 'the Spirit of God came upon them'; 'the Spirit of God moved them'; 'the Spirit of God spoke through them.' All these phrases indicate that some part of the believer's being, or personality, came under the Holy Spirit's control. But nowhere do we read in the Old Testament that the Holy Spirit ever came to take up His dwelling within the temple of a believer's physical body, thus taking control of his whole personality from within.

Third, the indwelling of the Christian by the Holy Spirit is **permanent.**

Under the Old Testament, believers experienced the visitation of the Holy Spirit in many different ways and at many different times. But in all these cases the Holy Spirit was always a Visitor, never a permanent Resident. In **John 14:16,** however, Jesus promised His disciples that when the Holy Spirit came to them, He would from then on abide with them for ever:

> *"And I will pray the Father, and He will give you another Helper* (the Holy Spirit), *that He may abide with you forever..."*

Thus we may characterise the gift of the Holy Spirit, as promised in the New Testament, by these three distinctive features: it is **personal;** it is an **indwelling;** it is **permanent.** Or, in one short phrase: it is a **personal, permanent indwelling.**

These distinctive features of the gift provide two reasons why it could not be given so long as Christ remained in bodily presence on earth.

First, while Christ was present on earth, He was the personal, authoritative representative of the Godhead. There was no need, and no place, for the Holy Spirit also to be personally present on earth at the same time. But after Christ's ascension into heaven, the way was then open for the Holy Spirit, in His turn, to come to earth as a Person.

It is now He, the Holy Spirit, who in this present dispensation is the personal representative of the Godhead here on earth.

Second, the gift of the Holy Spirit could not be given until after Christ's ascension, because the claim of every believer to receive it is in no way based upon his own merits, but simply and solely upon the merits of Christ's sacrificial death and resurrection. No one could receive the gift, therefore, until Christ's atoning work was complete and had received the approval of God the Father in heaven.

The Father's Promise

In **Galatians 3:13-14,** Paul links the promise of the Spirit directly to Christ's atonement:

> *Christ has redeemed us from the curse of the law, having become a curse for us (for it is written, "Cursed is everyone who hangs on a tree"),*
> *that the blessing of Abraham might come upon the Gentiles in Christ Jesus, **that we might receive the promise of the Spirit** through faith.*

Paul here establishes two facts of great interest and importance concerning the gift of the Holy Spirit to the Christian believer.

First of all, it is only through the redemptive work of Christ upon the cross that the believer may now receive the promise of the Spirit. In fact, this was one main purpose for which Christ suffered on the cross. He died and shed his blood that He might purchase thereby a twofold legal right: His own right to bestow, and the believer's right to receive, this precious gift of the Holy Spirit.

Thus, the receiving of the gift does not depend in any way upon the believer's own merits, but solely upon the all-sufficiency of Christ's atonement. It is through faith, not by works.

Second, we notice that Paul uses here the phrase, *the promise of the Spirit,* for he says: *that we might receive **the promise of the Spirit** through faith.* This agrees with the words which Jesus Himself uses in **Luke 24:49,** where He gives a final charge to His disciples, just before His ascension into heaven:

> *"Behold, I send the Promise of My Father upon you; but tarry in the city of Jerusalem until you are endued with power from on high."*

Jesus is here speaking to His disciples of the baptism in the Holy Spirit which they were to receive in the city of Jerusalem on the day of Pentecost. He uses two phrases to describe this experience. He calls it an enduement *with power from on high,* and also *the Promise of My Father.*

This second phrase, *the Promise of My Father,* gives us a wonderful insight into the mind and purpose of God the Father, concerning the gift of the Holy Spirit. Someone has conservatively estimated that the Bible contains seven thousand distinct promises, given by God to His believing people. But among all these seven thousand promises, Jesus singles out one from all the rest as being in a unique sense the Father's special promise for each of His believing children. What is this unique and special promise? It is what Paul calls *the promise of the Spirit.*

At Pentecost - on the very day the promise was fulfilled - Peter used a similar· form of speech, recorded in **Acts 2:38-39:**

> *"Repent, and let every one of you be baptised in the name of Jesus Christ for the remission of sins; and you shall receive the gift of the Holy Spirit.*
> *"For the promise is to you and to your children, and to all who are afar off, as many as the Lord our God will call."*

Peter here joins together the words 'gift' and 'promise.' To what special, promised gift does he refer? To the same as that spoken of by Jesus and by Paul - *the promise of the Spirit.* This is indeed *the Promise of the Father,* which He had planned and prepared through many long ages, that He might bestow it upon His believing children through Jesus Christ in this present dispensation.

In **Galatians 3:14** Paul also calls this promise *the blessing of Abraham.* Thus he links it with the supreme purpose of God in choosing Abraham for Himself.

In **Genesis 12:2-3,** when God first called Abraham out of Ur, He said:

> *"...I will bless you...*
> *And you shall be a blessing...*
> *And in you all the families of the earth shall be blessed."*

In His subsequent dealings with Abraham, God reaffirmed His purpose of blessing many times. For instance, in **Genesis 22:17-18:**

> *"In blessing I will bless you...*
> *In your seed all the nations of the earth shall be blessed..."*

To what specific blessing did all these promises of God look forward? The words of Paul in **Galatians 3:14** supply the answer: *the promise of the Spirit.* It was to purchase this blessing, promised to the seed of Abraham, that Jesus shed His blood on the cross.

Heaven's Seal On Christ's Atonement

However, the final consummation of Christ's atoning work did not come on earth, but in heaven. This is made plain in **Hebrews 9:11-12:**

> *But Christ came as High Priest of the good things to come, with the greater and more perfect tabernacle not made with hands, that is, not of this creation.*
> *Not with the blood of goats and calves, but with His own blood He entered the Most Holy Place once for all, having obtained eternal redemption.*

Farther on also, in **Hebrews 12:24,** we read that, as believers in the new covenant, we have come to,

> *Jesus the Mediator of the new covenant, and to the blood of sprinkling that speaks better things than that of Abel.*

These passages in Hebrews reveal that the atoning work of Christ was not finally consummated by the shedding of His blood upon the cross on earth, but by His later entering with His blood into the presence of the Father. There He presented that blood as the one final and sufficient satisfaction and expiation for all sin. It is this blood of

Christ, now sprinkled in heaven, that *speaks better things than that of Abel.*

The blood of Christ is contrasted with that of Abel in two main respects. First, Abel's blood was left sprinkled upon earth, while Christ's blood was presented and sprinkled in heaven. Second, Abel's blood called out to God for vengeance upon his murderer, while Christ's blood speaks to God in heaven for mercy and pardon.

This revelation, given in Hebrews, of Christ completing the atonement by presenting His own blood before the Father in heaven, enables us to understand why the gift of the Holy Spirit could not be given until Christ had been glorified. The Holy Spirit is given not upon the basis of the believer's own merits, but upon the basis of Christ's atonement.

This atonement was not finally consummated until the blood of Christ had been presented in heaven, and God the Father had declared His absolute satisfaction with this atoning sacrifice. Thereafter the giving of the Holy Spirit to those who believed in Christ was the public testimony of the supreme court of heaven that the blood of Christ was for ever accepted as an all-sufficient propitiation for all sin.

This is attested by the words of the apostle in **1 John 5:6,** where he says concerning Jesus:

> *This is He who came by water and blood - Jesus Christ; not only by water, but by water and blood. And it is the Spirit who bears witness, because the Spirit is truth.*

We see that the Holy Spirit bears witness to the blood of Jesus. In other words, the giving of the Holy Spirit to those who believe in Jesus constitutes the united testimony of the Father and the Spirit together to the all-sufficiency of the blood of Jesus to cleanse the believer from all sin.

This harmonises with what Peter says - in **Acts 2:33** - concerning the outpouring of the Holy Spirit on the day of Pentecost. Having first spoken of Christ's death and resurrection, Peter continues:

> *"Therefore being exalted to the right hand of God, and having received from the Father the promise of the Holy Spirit, He poured out this which you now see and hear."*

Christ first purchased man's redemption by His atoning death and resurrection. Then He ascended to His Father in heaven and there presented the blood which was the evidence and seal of redemption. Upon the Father's acceptance of the blood, Christ received from the Father the gift of the Holy Spirit to pour out upon those who believed in Him.

We may now sum up the revelation of Scripture concerning the plan of God to bestow upon all believers the gift of the Holy Spirit.

Implicit in God's choice of Abraham was the promise of the blessing of the Holy Spirit to all nations through Christ. By His blood shed upon the cross, Christ purchased for all believers the legal right to this blessing. After presenting His blood in heaven, Christ received from the Father the gift of the Holy Spirit. On the day of Pentecost, the Spirit Himself, who is the gift, was poured out from heaven upon the waiting believers on earth.

Thus, Father, Son and Holy Spirit were all three concerned in planning, purchasing and providing this, the supreme promise and the greatest of all gifts, for all God's believing people.

In the next chapter we shall view this same gift of the Holy Spirit from the human standpoint; and we shall consider what the conditions are which must be met in the life of each believer who desires to receive the gift.

Chapter 10

HOW TO RECEIVE THE HOLY SPIRIT

What are the conditions which must be fulfilled in the life of a person who desires to receive the gift of the Holy Spirit?

By Grace Through Faith

As we consider the teaching of Scripture on this subject, we shall find that there is one basic principle which applies alike to every provision made for man by the grace of God. It is stated in **Romans 11:6:**

And if by grace, then it is no longer of works; otherwise grace is no longer grace. But if it is of works, it is no longer grace; otherwise work is no longer work.

In this passage, as also elsewhere in his epistles, Paul contrasts the two expressions, 'grace' and 'works.' By 'grace,' Paul means always the free, unmerited favour and blessing of God, bestowed upon the undeserving, and even upon the ill-deserving. By 'works,' Paul means anything that a man may do, of his own ability, to earn for himself the blessing and favour of God.

Paul states that these two ways of receiving from God are mutually exclusive; they can never be combined. Whatever a man receives from God by grace is not of works; whatever a man receives from God by works is not of grace. Wherever grace operates, works are of no avail; wherever works operate, grace is of no avail.

This leads on to the further contrast between 'grace' and 'law,' stated in **John 1:17:**

> *For the law was given through Moses, but grace and truth came through Jesus Christ.*

Under the law of Moses, men sought to earn the blessing of God by what they did for themselves. Through Jesus Christ the free, unmerited blessing and favour of God are now offered to all men on the basis of what Christ has done on man's behalf. This is 'grace.'

All that we receive in this way from God through Jesus Christ is by grace; and the means by which we receive this grace is not by works, but by faith.

This is emphasised by Paul in **Ephesians 2:8-9:**

> *For by grace you have been saved through faith, and that not of yourselves; it is the gift of God, not of works, lest anyone should boast.*

The basic principle laid down by Paul in this passage can be summed up in three successive phrases: *by grace - through faith - not of works.* It applies in the receiving of every provision made for man by the grace of God.

Specifically, in **Galatians 3:13-14,** Paul applies the principle to the receiving of the gift of the Holy Spirit:

> *Christ has redeemed us from the curse of the law...that we might receive the promise of the Spirit through faith.*

Paul brings out two important and interrelated facts. First, the gift of the Holy Spirit is made available to man through the redemptive work of Christ upon the cross; that is to say, it is part of the total provision made for man by the grace of God through Jesus Christ. Second, this gift, like every other provision of God's grace, is received simply through faith, and not by works.

This question of how the gift of the Holy Spirit is received had apparently been raised amongst the Christian churches in Galatia, and Paul makes several references to it in the third chapter of his Epistle to the Galatians.

For instance, in **Galatians 3:2,** Paul says:

> *This only I want to learn from you: Did you receive the Spirit by the works of the law, or by the hearing of faith?*

Again, in verse **5** of the same chapter:

*Therefore He who supplies the Spirit to you...does He do it by the works of the law, or **by the hearing of faith?***

And again, in verse **14,** as we have already seen:

*...that we might receive the promise of the Spirit **through faith.***

Three times, therefore, in these few verses Paul emphasises that the receiving of the Spirit is by faith.

In other words, the basic essential preparation for believers to receive the Holy Spirit is that they should be instructed out of the Scriptures on the nature of God's provision for them, and how they may claim this provision through faith in the redemptive work of Christ on the cross. If this kind of scriptural instruction is first given, and received with faith by those seeking the Holy Spirit, there should thereafter be no need for great effort or delay in their receiving of the gift.

It would appear from Paul's Epistle to the Galatians that the Christians there had originally received from him with simple faith the message of the gospel and of the gift of the Holy Spirit, and had thus entered into the fulness of God's provision for them. Later, however, through other teachers, they had become involved in some kind of legalistic system, superimposed upon this gospel foundation, and had thus begun to lose their first vision of the simple receiving of God's gift by grace through faith.

One main purpose of Paul's epistle to them is to warn them of the dangers of this, and to call them back to the original simplicity of their faith.

It would seem that groups of Christians in various places today are being threatened by the same kind of error, against which Paul warned the Galatians. There is in many places today a tendency to impose some kind of system, or technique, upon those seeking the gift of the Holy Spirit.

The precise form of technique varies from group to group. In some places, the emphasis is upon some particular posture, or attitude. In other places, the emphasis is rather upon some special form of words, or the repetition of certain special phrases.

Instruction along these lines to those seeking the Holy Spirit is not necessarily unscriptural, but the great danger is that the particular posture, or form of words, instead of being merely a help to faith, may become a substitute for it. In this case, this kind of technique defeats its own ends. Instead of helping seekers to receive the Holy Spirit, it actually prevents them from doing so.

It is often as a result of this kind of technique that we meet the chronic seekers, who say: 'I've tried everything! I've tried praise; I've said Hallelujah; I've lifted my hands in the air; I've shouted; I've done everything - but it just doesn't work.' Without realising it, people who speak like this are making just the same error that the Galatians were slipping into: they are substituting works for faith, a technique for the simple hearing of God's Word.

What is the remedy? It is just that which Paul proposes to the Galatians: to return to *the hearing of faith*. Chronic seekers like these do not need more praise, or more shouting, or more lifting up of their hands. What they need is fresh instruction from God's Word on the free provisions of God's grace.

As a matter of general principle, wherever people are seeking the gift of the Holy Spirit, a period of instruction from God's Word should always precede any period of prayer. For my own part, if I were allotted a period of thirty minutes to help believers seeking the gift of the Holy Spirit, I should always wish to spend at least half that time - at least the first fifteen minutes - in giving scriptural instruction. Thereafter, the next fifteen minutes devoted to prayer would produce far more positive results than a full thirty minutes given to prayer, without any instruction beforehand.

We see, then, that the basic requirement for receiving the gift of the Holy Spirit is defined by Paul as *the hearing of faith.*

However, in laying down this principle, we must be careful to guard against a false interpretation of what is meant by faith. Faith is not a substitute for obedience. On the contrary, true faith is always manifested in obedience. Thus obedience becomes both the test, and the evidence, of faith.

This applies as much to the receiving of the Holy Spirit as in any other area of God's grace.

In his defence to the Jewish Council, in **Acts 5:32,** Peter focuses upon obedience as the proper expression of faith:

> *"And we are His witnesses to these things, and so also is the Holy Spirit **whom God has given to those who obey Him."***

In speaking of the gift of the Holy Spirit, Paul stresses faith, while Peter stresses obedience. There is, however, no conflict between the two. True faith is always linked with obedience. Complete faith results in complete obedience. Peter says here that when our obedience is complete, the gift of the Holy Spirit is ours.

Six Steps Of Faith

In seeking the gift of the Holy Spirit, how should complete obedience be expressed? We find six steps set forth in Scripture, which mark the pathway of obedience leading to the gift of the Holy Spirit.

Repentance And Baptism

The first two steps are stated by the apostle Peter in **Acts 2:38:**

> *"Repent, and let every one of you be baptised in the name of Jesus Christ for the remission of sins; and you shall receive the gift of the Holy Spirit."*

The two steps here stated by Peter are, first, *Repent;* and second, *be baptised.*

Repentance is an inward change of heart and attitude towards God, that opens the way for the sinner to be reconciled with God. Thereafter, baptism is an outward act by which the believer testifies to the inward change wrought by God's grace in his heart.

Thirsting

The third step on this pathway to the fulness of the Holy Spirit is stated by Jesus in **John 7:37-38**:

"If anyone thirsts, let him come to Me and drink.
He who believes in Me, as the Scripture has said, out
of his heart will flow rivers of living water."

In the next verse, the writer of the Gospel goes on to explain that this promise of Jesus refers to the gift of the Holy Spirit.

This agrees with what Jesus says also in **Matthew 5:6**:

"Blessed are those who hunger and thirst for
righteousness,
For they shall be filled."

One essential condition for receiving the fulness of the Holy Spirit is to be hungry and thirsty. God does not squander His blessings on those who feel no need for them. Many professing Christians who lead good, respectable lives never receive the fulness of the Holy Spirit simply because they feel no need for it. They are satisfied without this blessing, and God leaves them that way.

From the human point of view, it quite often happens that those who seem least deserving receive the gift of the Holy Spirit, and those who seem most deserving do not. This is explained by the words in **Luke 1:53**:

He (God) has filled the hungry with good things,
And the rich He has sent away empty.

God responds to our sincere inner longings, but He is not impressed by our religious profession.

Asking

In **Luke 11:13** Jesus presents the fourth step to receiving the Holy Spirit:

"If you then, being evil, know how to give good gifts
to your children, how much more will your heavenly
Father give the Holy Spirit to those who ask Him!"

Here Jesus places upon God's children an obligation to ask their heavenly Father for the gift of the Holy Spirit. We sometimes hear Christians make some such remark as this: 'If God wants me to have the Holy Spirit, He will give it to me. I do not need to ask Him for it.' However, this attitude is not scriptural. Jesus plainly teaches that God's children should ask their heavenly Father for this special gift of the Holy Spirit.

Drinking

After asking, the next step is receiving. In **John 7:37,** Jesus calls this *drinking,* for He says:

"If anyone thirsts, let him come to Me and drink."

'Drinking' represents an active process of receiving. The infilling of the Holy Spirit cannot be received by a merely negative, or passive attitude. No one can drink except of his own active volition; and no one can drink with a closed mouth. As it is in the natural, so it is in the spiritual.

In **Psalm 81:10,** the Lord says:

Open your mouth wide, and I will fill it.

God cannot fill a closed mouth. Simple though it may seem, there are those who fail to receive the fulness of the Spirit, simply because they fail to open their mouth.

Yielding

After drinking, the sixth and last step to receive the fulness of the Holy Spirit is **yielding.**

In **Romans 6:13,** Paul speaks to Christians of a twofold surrender to God:

*...but present **yourselves** to God as being alive from the dead, and **your members** as instruments of righteousness to God.*

Two successive stages are here set before us as Christians. The first surrender is of *yourselves* - the surrender of the will and of the personality. However, this is not all. There is a further degree of surrender, in which we surrender not merely our will, but our physical *members.*

To make this further degree of surrender requires a much greater measure of confidence in God. In yielding ourselves - our wills - we yield obedience to the revealed will of God, but we still retain the exercise of our own understanding. We are willing to do what God asks of us, provided that we first understand what is asked.

However, in yielding our physical members we go beyond this. We no longer seek even to understand intellectually what God asks of us. We merely hand over unreserved control of our physical members and allow God to use them according to His own will and purpose, without demanding to understand what God is doing, or why He is doing it.

It is only as we make this second surrender, that we come to the place of total, unconditional yieldedness. And it is just at this very point that the Holy Spirit comes in in His fulness and takes control of our members.

The particular member of which He takes full control is that unruly member which no man can tame - the tongue. Thus the yielding of our tongue to the Spirit of God to control within us according to His own will, and apart from the exercise of our own intellectual understanding, marks the climax of yieldedness - of surrender - of complete obedience. It is by this that we receive the gift of the Holy Spirit.

We have outlined the following six successive steps to receiving the fulness of the Holy Spirit: first, repentance; second, being baptised; third, being thirsty; fourth, asking; fifth, drinking - that is, actively receiving; sixth, yielding - that is, surrendering control of our physical members, apart from the exercise of our intellectual understanding.

Out of this outline, the question will naturally arise: is it necessarily true that every person who receives the gift of the Holy Spirit has completely followed through all the six steps just outlined?

The answer to this question is - no. God's grace is sovereign. Wherever God sees fit, He is free to reach out in grace to needy souls beyond the conditions actually set forth in His Word. God's grace is not necessarily limited by the conditions which He Himself imposes. But on the other hand, wherever those conditions are fully met, God's faithfulness will never withhold the blessing which He has promised.

It would seem that of the steps just outlined, there are some which are sometimes omitted by people who nevertheless do receive the gift of the Holy Spirit. In particular, the gift of the Holy Spirit is at times granted to people who have not been baptised, and who have never specifically asked God for this gift.

I know that this is so, because it happened in my own experience. I myself received the gift of the Holy Spirit before I was baptised, and without ever specifically asking for it. In these two points, God reached out to me in His free and sovereign grace beyond the conditions actually imposed in His Word. I realise, however, that on my side, this now makes me just so much the more a debtor to God's grace. It certainly opens no door to me for pride, carelessness, or disobedience.

It would seem, however, that God never bestows the gift of the Holy Spirit where the other four conditions, stated in His Word, are not fulfilled. That is, God never bestows the Holy Spirit where there is not, first of all, repentance; and then, after that, a spiritual thirst, and a willingness both to receive, and to yield.

In concluding this series of studies on the baptism in the Holy Spirit, it will be appropriate to emphasise once again the close connection between the fulness of the Holy Spirit and obedience. As Peter says, the gift of the Holy Spirit is for those who obey God. Even where God in His grace bestows this gift upon those who have not yet fully met the conditions of His Word, this still leaves no room for carelessness, or disobedience.

In **Acts 10,** we read that as Peter preached in the house of Cornelius, the Holy Spirit fell upon all those who heard his word. However, the record of Acts makes it clear that this demonstration of God's grace was in no sense to be interpreted as a substitute for obedience to God's Word, for we read in verse **48:**

> ...he (Peter) *commanded them to be baptised...*

Even for those who have received the gift of the Holy Spirit, the ordinance of baptism in water still remains a commandment of God's Word that may not be set aside.

Above all, in this realm of spiritual gifts, we need to be continually on our guard against spiritual pride. The more richly we receive of the gifts of God's grace, the greater is our obligation to be obedient and faithful in the exercise and stewardship of these gifts.

This principle of responsibility for grace received is summed up by the words of Jesus concerning stewardship, in **Luke 12:48:**

> *"...For everyone to whom much is given, from him much will be required; and to whom much has been committed, of him they will ask the more."*

The more abundantly we receive of God's gifts and graces through Jesus Christ, the greater becomes our obligation to humility, to consecration, and to unfailing obedience.

Chapter 11

IN THE CLOUD AND IN THE SEA

Throughout the foregoing ten chapters we have been considering that part of Christian doctrine which is called, in **Hebrews 6:2,** *the doctrine of baptisms.*

We took note of the fact that there are actually four distinct types of baptism referred to in the New Testament. These are: first, the baptism of John the Baptist; second, Christian baptism in water; third, the baptism of suffering; fourth, the baptism in the Holy Spirit.

Of these four types of baptism, the two which are most directly related to the experience of all Christian believers in this dispensation are the second and the fourth: that is, Christian baptism in water and the baptism in the Holy Spirit. For this reason, we have concentrated our attention mainly on these two forms of baptism.

The time has now come to view these in perspective; that is, to see how they are related to each other, and to the other parts of God's plan and provision for Christians. We may put the question in this form: what part do baptism in water and the baptism in the Holy Spirit play in the total plan of God for all New Testament believers?

We shall follow an approach to this question frequently employed by the writers of the New Testament: that is, we shall view God's deliverance of Israel out of Egypt as a 'type,' or a pattern, of the greater deliverance from the slavery of sin and of Satan offered to the whole human race through Jesus Christ. We shall focus on three specific features of the deliverance of Israel out of Eygpt; and we shall use these to illustrate three main elements in the salvation provided for all men through Christ.

111

Salvation Through Blood

First of all, God sent His appointed deliverer, Moses, to Israel right where they were, in the midst of Egypt, and in the midst of their misery and slavery. There He saved them from wrath and from judgment through their faith in the blood of the sacrifice which He had appointed - that is, the passover lamb.

In the New Testament, in **John 1:29,** John the Baptist - the forerunner sent to prepare the way before Christ - introduced Him with the words: *"Behold! The Lamb of God who takes away the sin of the world!"* Thus he proclaimed Jesus as the appointed Saviour, whose sacrificial death and shed blood would accomplish all that had been foreshadowed by the passover lamb.

Later, in **1 Corinthians 5:7,** looking back on Christ's death and resurrection, Paul says: *...Christ, our Passover, was sacrificed for us.*

As a natural type, the passover lamb provided temporary deliverance for Israel from physical slavery. The sacrifice of the divine antitype, Jesus Christ, provided eternal salvation for all who put their faith in His shed blood as the propitiation for their sins.

It was not God's purpose, however, for Israel to remain any longer in Egypt. The very same night that the passover was sacrificed, Israel began their exodus, no longer a rabble of slaves, but now an army in ordered ranks. There was urgency in all that they did. They took their bread before it was leavened. They marched in haste, with their loins girded, and their staves in their hands.

In like manner, God meets the sinner right where he is in the world, and saves him in the depths of his need and bondage. But God does not leave the sinner there. Immediately He calls him out into a totally new way of life - a life of separation and sanctification.

A Double Baptism

The next two stages in Israel's deliverance out of Egypt are described by Paul in **1 Corinthians 10:1-4:.**

*Moreover, brethren, I do not want you to be unaware
that all our fathers were under the cloud, all passed
through the sea,
all were baptised into Moses in the cloud and in the sea,
all ate the same spiritual food,
and all drank the same spiritual drink. For they drank
of that spiritual Rock that followed them, and that Rock
was Christ.*

Just a little further on in the same chapter, Paul relates
these experiences of Israel in the Old Testament to corresponding experiences of Christians in the New Testament.

For he says, in verse **6:**

Now these things became our examples...

And again, in verse **11:**

Now all these things happened to them as examples
(as types - or patterns of behaviour), *and they were
written for our admonition,* (that is, to instruct and
to warn us) *on whom the ends of the ages have come*
(that is, for us who now live in this the closing
dispensation of the present age).

In other words, Paul says, these experiences of Israel
in the Old Testament are not merely interesting historical
events in the past, but they also contain an urgent and important message for us as Christians in this age. They are
specially recorded, by divine direction, as examples, or
patterns of behaviour, which God intends to be carefully
followed by all Christian believers in this dispensation.

With this in mind, let us now turn back to the first four
verses of the chapter, and let us consider carefully just what
are the examples, or the lessons, which Paul there sets before
us.

First of all, we notice that, in these four verses, that very
short but important word 'all' occurs no less than five times.

Paul says:

*...**all** our fathers were under the cloud, **all** passed
through the sea,
all were baptised into Moses in the cloud and in the sea,
all ate the same spiritual food,
and **all** drank the same spiritual drink...*

113

Clearly, Paul is emphasising that all these examples, or patterns, are to be followed by all God's believing people. God does not leave room for any exceptions. These things are for all His people.

What are the particular patterns to which Paul here refers? There are four successive experiences: first, all were under the cloud; second, all passed through the sea; third, all ate the same spiritual food; fourth, all drank the same spiritual drink.

These then are four pattern experiences which are to be followed by all God's people: first, passing under the cloud; second, passing through the sea; third, eating the same spiritual food; fourth, drinking the same spiritual drink.

To what do these four patterns correspond in the experience of believers in this dispensation? What is their lesson for us, as Christians today?

We notice, first of all, that these four experiences naturally fall into two distinct pairs. The first two - passing under the cloud and through the sea - were single experiences, that occurred only once. The second two - eating and drinking spiritual food and drink - were continuing experiences that were regularly repeated over a long period of time.

Let us begin with the first pair of experiences - those that took place only once: passing under the cloud and through the sea.

The key to understanding these is provided by a distinctive phrase which Paul uses in connection with them. He says: *all were baptised into Moses in the cloud and in the sea.*

Plainly, therefore, these two experiences correspond to two forms of baptism, both of which God has ordained for all Christians in this dispensation.

What are the two forms of baptism represented by these two experiences?

In the light of our previous studies, it is now easy for us to supply the answer to this question. The baptism in the cloud for Israel corresponds to the baptism in the Holy Spirit for the Christian. The baptism in the sea for Israel corresponds to baptism in water for the Christian.

If we now examine the details of these two experiences of Israel, as related in the Old Testament, we shall see just how appropriate each of them is as a pattern of the corresponding experience for Christians today.

For the historical account of Israel passing under the cloud and through the sea we must turn to Exodus, chapters 13 and 14. These two chapters relate how, after the sacrifice of the passover lamb in Egypt, the people of Israel began their exodus from Egypt the same night; and how they came to the waters of the Red Sea and miraculously passed through, as on dry land.

The first mention of their passing under the cloud is found in **Exodus 13:20-21:**

> *So they took their journey from Succoth and camped in Etham at the edge of the wilderness.*
> *And the Lord went before them by day in a pillar of cloud to lead the way, and by night in a pillar of fire to give them light, so as to go by day and night.*

Referring to this in **1 Corinthians** 10 Paul says, *all our fathers were under the cloud.* This leads us to understand that, at a certain point on Israel's journey out of Egypt, this unique, supernatural cloud came down over them from above, and thereafter continued to rest over them.

It is clear that this cloud was sensibly perceptible to Israel, and that it took two different forms. By day, it was a cloud, giving shadow from the heat of the sun. By night, it was a pillar of fire, giving both light and warmth in the darkness and coldness of the night. By day and by night alike, it provided Israel with divine direction and guidance.

If we now turn on into **Exodus 14,** we find there two further facts revealed about his wonderful cloud. First, God Himself - the LORD - Jehovah - was personally present within the cloud. Secondly, this cloud served both to separate, and to protect, Israel from the Egyptians.

These facts are recorded in **Exodus 14:19-20:**

> *And the Angel of God, who went before the camp of Israel, moved and went behind them; and the pillar of cloud went from before them and stood behind them.*
> *So it came between the camp of the Egyptians and the*

camp of Israel. Thus it was a cloud and darkness to the one, (that is, to the Egyptians), *and it gave light by night to the other* (that is, to Israel), *so that the one did not come near the other all that night.*

A little further on, in verse **24** of the same chapter, we read again about the cloud:

Now it came to pass, in the morning watch, that the LORD looked down upon the army of the Egyptians through the pillar of fire and cloud, and He troubled the army of the Egyptians.

From this account we see that the LORD Himself - Jehovah - the great Angel of God - was in the cloud, and moved in the cloud. It was in the cloud that He moved over Israel from their front to their rear, and in the cloud that He interposed His own presence between Israel and the Egyptians, to separate and to protect His own people from their enemies.

We see, too, that the cloud had a very different meaning and effect for Israel, from that which it had for the Egyptians. For the Egyptians, *it was a cloud and darkness;* but to Israel *it gave light by night.* This cloud was darkness to Egypt, the people of this world; but it was light to Israel, the people of God.

Furthermore, when daylight came, the effect of the cloud was even more fearful for the Egyptians. For we read:

...in the morning watch, that the LORD looked down upon the army of the Egyptians through the pillar of fire and cloud, and He troubled the army of the Egyptians.

We have said that this cloud under which Israel passed, and in which they were baptised, is a type, or picture, of the baptism in the Holy Spirit. Let us now set out briefly, in order, the facts which we know about this cloud; and let us see how accurately and how perfectly each one of them applies to the baptism in the Holy Spirit.

Here, then, are the main facts revealed about the cloud.

First, this cloud came down over God's people from above, out of heaven.

Second, it was not merely an invisible influence, but it was sensibly perceptible.

Third, it provided shadow from the heat by day, and light and warmth by night.

Fourth, it gave God's people divine direction and guidance throughout their journeyings.

Fifth, within the cloud was the actual, personal presence of the LORD, Jehovah, Himself, and it was in the cloud that the Lord came personally to the rescue of His people from their enemies.

Sixth, the cloud gave light to the people of God, but to their enemies the same cloud was something dark and fearful.

Seventh, the cloud came between God's people and their enemies, thus separating and protecting them.

Let us now see how perfectly each one of these facts sets forth an important aspect of truth concerning the baptism in the Holy Spirit and what this experience means for God's people in this dispensation.

First, the baptism in the Holy Spirit is the glorious, personal presence of God Himself coming down over God's people from heaven, enveloping and immersing them.

Second, the baptism in the Holy Spirit is not merely an invisible influence, but it is something which is sensibly perceptible, and the effects which it produces can be both seen and heard.

Third, the Holy Spirit, coming in this way, is the appointed Comforter of God's people; He provides shade from heat, light and warmth in the midst of darkness and cold.

Fourth, the Holy Spirit provides God's people with divine direction and guidance throughout their earthly pilgrimage.

Fifth, within this experience is contained the actual presence of the Lord Himself, for Jesus says concerning it, in **John 14:18:**

> *"I will not leave you orphans; I* (myself personally)
> *will come to you."*

Sixth, the baptism in the Holy Spirit brings a heavenly light to the people of God; but to the people of this world this supernatural experience remains something dark, incomprehensible, even fearful. As Paul says in **1 Corinthians 2:14:**

> ...*the natural man does not receive the things of the Spirit of God, for they are foolishness to him; nor can he know them, because they are spiritually discerned.*

Seventh, the baptism in the Holy Spirit, as a spiritual experience, marks a decisive separation between the people of God and the people of this world; it both separates and protects God's people from the sinful, corrupting influences of this world.

So much for *the baptism in the cloud.* Let us now turn to *the baptism in the sea.* This experience of Israel passing through the Red Sea is described in the same fourteenth chapter of Exodus.

In **Exodus 14:21-22,** we read:

> *Then Moses stretched out his hand over the sea; and the Lord caused the sea to go back by a strong east wind all that night, and made the sea into dry land, and the waters were divided.*
> *So the children of Israel went into the midst of the sea on the dry ground, and the waters were a wall to them on their right hand and on their left.*

After this we read how the Egyptians attempted to follow Israel through the Red Sea; and the culmination of the whole experience, with the final overthrow of the Egyptians, is related in verse **27:**

> *And Moses stretched out his hand over the sea; and when the morning appeared, the sea returned to its full depth, while the Egyptians were fleeing into it. So the Lord overthrew the Egyptians in the midst of the sea.*

Side by side with this account in Exodus, we should also read the inspired comment of Scripture, given in **Hebrews 11:29:**

> **By faith** *they* (that is, Israel) *passed through the Red Sea as by dry land, whereas the Egyptians, attempting to do so, were drowned.*

In the light of these passages, we can now set out

briefly the main facts revealed about the passing of Israel through the Red Sea; and we can see how accurately and how perfectly each of them applies to Christian baptism in water.

First, the passing of Israel through the Red Sea was made possible only through a supernatural provision of God's power.

Second, Israel could avail themselves of this provision only by their own faith; the waters were both opened and closed again by an act of faith on the part of Moses, and Israel as a whole were able to pass through only by faith.

Third, the Egyptians, attempting to do the same thing, but without faith, were not saved, but destroyed.

Fourth, Israel went down into the waters, passed through the waters, and came up again out of the waters.

Fifth, by passing through the waters Israel were finally separated from their last direct contact with Egypt, and from the last threat of Egypt's dominion over them.

Sixth, Israel came up out of the waters to follow a new leader, to live by new laws and to march to a new destination.

Let us now see how perfectly each one of these facts illustrates an important aspect of truth concerning Christian baptism in water, and what this experience means for God's people in this dispensation.

First, Christian baptism in water has been made possible for the believer only through the death and supernatural resurrection of Jesus Christ.

Second, Christian baptism is effectual only through personal faith on the part of the believer: *he who believes and is baptised will be saved.*

Third, those who observe this ordinance without personal faith are like the Egyptians entering the Red Sea: their act does not save them; it destroys them.

Fourth, in every case where baptism in water is described in the New Testament, the person being baptised went down into the water, passed through the water, and came up out of the water again.

Fifth, baptism in water is intended by God to separate

the believer from the world, and from the continuing dominion of the world over him.

Sixth, the believer after baptism is directed by God into a new kind of life, with a new leader, new laws and a new destination. Paul emphasises this 'newness' in **Romans 6:4:**

Therefore we were buried with Him through baptism into death, that just as Christ was raised from the dead by the glory of the Father, even so we also should walk in newness of life.

We have seen that, in the course of their deliverance from Egypt, God's people under the Old Testament shared in two experiences common to them all: they all passed under the cloud and through the sea; they were all baptised in the cloud and in the sea. Let us now consider briefly the place that these two experiences occupied in God's total plan of salvation for His people.

God began the work of delivering His people where they were, in Egypt, through their faith in the blood of the passover sacrifice. However, once God had saved his people in Egypt, He no longer allowed them to remain there. On the contrary, He called them to march out the very same night of their deliverance, in haste, with their loins girded, no longer a mere rabble of slaves, but now an army of men prepared for war.

When the Egyptians proceeded to march after Israel, intent upon bringing them back into bondage again, God's next two stages of deliverance for His people consisted in making them pass under the cloud and through the sea. By these two experiences God achieved two main purposes for His people. First, He completed their deliverance out of Egypt's bondage; second, He made the necessary provision for the new life into which He was leading them.

We have already pointed out that all these things are examples, or patterns, of God's plan of deliverance for His people in this present dispensation. Immediately after the initial experience of salvation, God still today calls the sinner out from his old life, his old habits and associations. This call of God to come out and be separate is just as clear as

God's call to Israel to come out of Egypt; for Paul says to Christians in **2 Corinthians 6:17-18:**

> *"...Come out from among them*
> *And be separate, says the Lord,*
> *Do not touch what is unclean,*
> *And I will receive you.*
> *I will be a Father to you,*
> *And you shall be My sons and daughters,*
> *Says the Lord Almighty."*

Still today also, Satan, the god of this world, seeks to do as Pharaoh did - to follow after God's people, as they move out from his dominion, and to bring them back again under his bondage.

Because of this, God has made for His believing people today a double provision corresponding to the double baptism of Israel in the cloud and in the sea. God has ordained that, after salvation through faith in the blood of Christ, all His believing people should thereafter be baptised both in water and in the Holy Spirit.

By this double baptism, it is God's intention that His people should be finally delivered from the association and the dominion of this world; and that the way back into the old life should thenceforth for ever be closed behind them. By this double baptism, also, God makes the provision necessary for the new life into which He thereafter intends to lead His people.

Spiritual Food And Drink

Let us now consider briefly the other two experiences which God ordained for all His people under the Old Testament: that is, eating the same spiritual food, and drinking the same spiritual drink. Unlike the double baptism, which was never repeated, the food and drink represented an ongoing provision of God, of which His people had to partake regularly every day, until they had completed their pilgrimage.

The spiritual food which God ordained for all Israel was the manna which came down to them regularly each morning. It was mainly upon this supernatural form of food that Israel lived throughout the forty years of their pilgrimage through the wilderness.

Speaking of this in the New Testament, Paul describes it as *spiritual food*. In other words, Paul indicates that, for us as Christians in this dispensation, this manna corresponds not to the natural material food with which we must feed out bodies, but to the spiritual, supernatural food with which we must feed our souls.

What, then, is this spiritual, supernatural food of the Christian?

The answer is given by Christ in **Matthew 4:4:**

> *"...It is written, 'Man shall not live by bread alone, but by every word that proceeds from the mouth of God.'"*

The spiritual food, appointed by God for all believers in this dispensation, is God's own Word.

As we feed by faith upon the written Word of God, the Scriptures, we receive within ourselves the divine life of the personal Word, that is, Jesus Christ Himself. For Jesus said also of Himself, in **John 6:51:**

> *"I am the living bread which came down from heaven..."*

Thus, it is through the written Word that the personal Word, the living bread from heaven, comes down to nourish the soul of the believer.

The ordinances for the gathering of manna by Israel are stated in **Exodus 16.** There are three main points: first, it was gathered regularly; second, it was gathered individually; third, it was gathered early in the day.

The same three principles apply to the believer in this dispensation. Each Christian needs to feed upon God's Word regularly, individually and early in the day.

Finally, there is the appointed spiritual drink of God's people. For Israel in the Old Testament, this drink was a river that flowed out of a Rock; and Paul tells us, *that Rock was Christ.*

For the Christian, the divinely appointed drink is the river of the Holy Spirit flowing forth from within his own inner being. For Christ says in **John 7:37-38,** speaking of the Holy Spirit:

"...If anyone thirsts, let him come to Me and drink.
He who believes in Me, as the Scripture has said, out
of his heart will flow rivers of living water."

For Israel in the Old Testament this river flowed out of a smitten Rock; for the Christian today this river flows out of the smitten side of the Saviour, for it was His atoning death upon the cross that purchased for all believers the indwelling fulness of the Holy Spirit.

The initial baptism in the Holy Spirit is a once-for-all experience that never needs to be repeated. But drinking from the river of the Spirit that now flows from within is something that each believer needs to do just as regularly as Israel drank from the rock in the desert.

For this reason, Paul uses a continuing tense when he says, in **Ephesians 5:18:** *be* (continually) *filled* (and refilled) *with the Spirit...* Continual drinking in of the Spirit leads to the outward expressions Paul describes in the next two verses:

...speaking to one another in psalms and hymns and
spiritual songs, singing and making melody in your
heart to the Lord,
giving thanks always for all things to God the Father
in the name of our Lord Jesus Christ...

Continual feeding on God's Word and drinking of God's Spirit are essential for a life of continuing victory and fruitfulness. Israel would inevitably have perished in the wilderness without their daily portion of manna from heaven and living water from the rock. The believer today is no less dependent upon the daily manna of God's Word and the daily filling, and refilling, of God's Spirit.

Let us now apply the complete pattern to the experience of the Christian in this dispensation.

God has ordained for each believer today five experiences, each typified by an experience of Israel in the Old Testament.

These five experiences are as follows: salvation through faith in the blood of Jesus Christ; baptism in the Holy

Spirit; baptism in water; daily feeding upon God's Word; daily drinking of God's Spirit from within.

Of these five experiences, the first three - salvation, and baptism in water and in the Spirit - are experiences that occur only once, and need not be repeated. The last two - feeding upon God's Word and drinking of God's Spirit - are experiences which the believer must continue to practise regularly each day throughout his earthly pilgrimage.

Book 4

PURPOSES OF PENTECOST

But the manifestation of the Spirit is given to each one for the profit of all... **1 Corinthians 12:7**

BOOK 4:
PURPOSES OF PENTECOST

TABLE OF CONTENTS

Section C: THE SPIRIT-FILLED PREACHER

Chapter 1

INTRODUCTION AND WARNING

In chapter 10 of Book 3 we considered the practical steps of faith and obedience by which a person may enter into the baptism in the Holy Spirit. Leading on from that is a further practical question which we shall consider in this book: for what purposes is the baptism in the Holy Spirit given? Or to put it another way: what results does God desire to produce in the life of the believer through baptising him in the Holy Spirit?

Before giving a positive, scriptural answer to this question, however, it is first of all necessary to clear up certain common misunderstandings which often trouble people who have newly received the baptism in the Spirit, and which thus prevent them from receiving the full benefits and blessings God intended for them through this experience.

The Holy Spirit Is Not A Dictator

The first point which needs to be emphasised is that, in the life of the believer, the Holy Spirit never plays the role of a dictator.

When Jesus promised the gift of the Holy Spirit to His disciples, He spoke of Him in terms such as 'Helper,' 'Comforter,' 'Guide,' or 'Teacher.' The Holy Spirit always keeps Himself within these limits. He never usurps the will or the personality of the believer. He never in any sense forces or compels the believer to do anything against the believer's own will or choice.

The Holy Spirit is called in **Hebrews 10:29,** *the Spirit of grace.* He is far too gracious to impose Himself upon the

129

believer, or to force His way into any area of the believer's personality where He is not received as a welcome guest.

In **2 Corinthians 3:17** Paul emphasises the freedom that proceeds from the Holy Spirit:

> *Now the Lord is the Spirit; and where the Spirit of the Lord is, there is liberty* (freedom).

In **Romans 8:15,** Paul contrasts this freedom of the Spirit-baptised Christian believer with the bondage of Israel to the law in the Old Testament, and he reminds Christians:

> *For you did not receive the spirit of bondage* (slavery) *again to fear...*

It follows therefore that the extent to which the Holy Spirit will control and direct the believer is the extent to which the believer himself will voluntarily yield to the Holy Spirit, and accept the Holy Spirit's control and direction. In **John 3:34,** John the Baptist says:

> *"...for God does not give the Spirit by measure."*

The measure is not in God's giving; the measure is in our receiving. We may have as much of the Holy Spirit as we are willing to receive. But in order to receive Him, we must voluntarily yield to Him and accept His control. He will never force us to yield, or to do anything else, against our own will.

Some believers make just this mistake at the time of seeking the baptism in the Holy Spirit. They imagine that the Holy Spirit will move them so forcefully that they will be literally compelled to speak with other tongues, without any act of their own will. However, this will never happen.

In **Acts 2:4,** we read, concerning the first disciples on the day of Pentecost:

> *And they were all filled with the Holy Spirit and* (they) *began to speak with other tongues, as the Spirit gave them utterance.*

We notice here that the disciples first began to speak themselves, and then the Holy Spirit gave them utterance. If the disciples had never voluntarily begun to speak, the Holy Spirit would never have given them utterance. He would never have forced utterance upon them without their own voluntary cooperation. In this matter of speaking with other tongues, there must be cooperation on the part of the believer with the Holy Spirit.

Someone has summed up this two-way relationship between the Holy Spirit and the believer as follows: the believer **cannot** do it without the Holy Spirit; the Holy Spirit **will not** do it without the believer.

This cooperation of the believer with the Holy Spirit continues to be just as necessary even after receiving the baptism in the Holy Spirit. Here again some believers make a great mistake in supposing that, after they have once received the initial infilling of the Holy Spirit, with the evidence of speaking with tongues, thereafter the Holy Spirit will automatically go on to exercise full control of their whole being, without any further response or cooperation on their part. But this is far from being true.

We have already quoted the words of Paul in **2 Corinthians 3:17:** *Now the Lord is the Spirit.* The Holy Spirit is indeed Lord - just as fully as God the Father and God the Son. But He, like the Father and the Son, waits for the believer to acknowledge His Lordship.

In order to make the Lordship of the Spirit an effective reality in his daily life, the believer must continually yield to the Spirit's control over every area of his personality and every department of his life. Someone has very truly said that it requires at least as much faith, consecration, and prayer to keep filled with the Spirit as it required to receive the initial infilling.

The baptism in the Holy Spirit is not the final goal to be attained in Christian experience; it is an initial gateway leading into a new realm of Christian living. After entering in through this gateway, each believer has a personal responsibility to press on with faith and determination, and to explore for himself all the wonderful potentialities of this new realm into which he has entered.

The believer who fails to realise and apply this truth will experience few, if any, of the benefits or blessings which God intended for him through the baptism in the Holy Spirit. In all probability, such a believer will become a disappointment and a stumbling block, both to himself and to other Christians.

Utilising God's Total Provision

This leads us naturally to another area of misunderstanding which must be cleared up. A careful study of the New Testament makes it plain that God has made full provision to meet every need of every believer, in every area of his being and in every aspect of his experience. As clear proof of this, we may cite two very powerful Scriptures from the New Testament:

2 Corinthians 9:8:

> *And God is able to make all grace abound toward you, that you, always having all sufficiency in all things, have an abundance for every good work.*

And again, **2 Peter 1:3:**

> *...His* (God's) *divine power has given to us all things that pertain to life and godliness, through the knowledge of Him who called us by glory and virtue...*

These Scriptures reveal that God's grace and power combined, through the knowledge of Jesus Christ, have already made an absolutely full and complete provision for every need of every believer. There is no need of any kind that can ever arise in any area of a believer's life, or personality, for which God has not already made a perfect provision through Jesus Christ.

If we now go on to consider the various different parts of God's total provision for the believer, we find that they are manifold and various; and that one part of God's provision is not a substitute for any other part. It is just here that so many believers make a serious mistake: they try to make one part of God's provision serve as a substitute for some other part. But God never intended it to be that way, and therefore it does not work.

As a clear, practical example of God's provision for the

believer, we may consider the list of spiritual armour, given by Paul in **Ephesians 6.**

In **Ephesians 6:11,** Paul says:

Put on the whole armour of God...

And again in verse **13:**

Therefore take up the whole armour of God...

In both these verses Paul emphasises that, for full protection, the Christian must put on the complete armour, not just a few parts of it. In the next four verses, Paul then goes on to enumerate the following six items of armour: the girdle of truth; the breastplate of righteousness; the shoes of the preparation of the gospel; the shield of faith; the helmet of salvation; the sword of the Spirit.

It is obvious that the Christian who avails himself of the all these six items of armour is fully protected from the crown of his head to the soles of his feet. On the other hand, if he omits only one part of the armour, his protection immediately ceases to be complete.

For example, if a Christian puts on all the other five items, but leaves off the helmet, he is liable to be wounded in the head; and once wounded there, his ability to make use of the rest of the armour will be impaired. Conversely, a Christian might put on the helmet and all the rest of the armour for the body, but omit the shoes. In this case, his ability to march over rough ground would be affected, and thus his total usefulness as a soldier would be impaired. Or again, a Christian might put on all the five items of defensive armour, but fail to carry the sword. In this case, he would have no means of keeping his enemy at a distance, or of pressing home an active attack against him.

We see therefore that, for full protection, a Christian must put on all the different items of armour which God has provided. He cannot omit any one piece, and expect that another piece will serve as a substitute. God does not intend it that way. He has provided a complete set of armour, and He expects the Christian to put it all on.

The same principle applies to the whole of God's provision for the Christian. In **Colossians 4:12,** Paul records the prayer of Epaphras for the Christians at Colosse, that they *may stand perfect and complete in all the will of God.* In order to stand thus perfect and complete in the fulness of God's will, a Christian must avail himself of all that God has provided for him through Christ. He cannot omit any part of God's total provision, and then expect that some other part of God's provision will serve as a substitute for that part which has been omitted.

Yet it is just at this point that so many Christians go astray in their thinking. Consciously, or unconsciously, they reason that because they know they have availed themselves of some parts of God's provision for them, they do not need to concern themselves about other parts which they have omitted.

We may give some common examples of the incomplete Christian experience which this kind of reasoning produces.

For instance, some Christians lay great emphasis upon witnessing by word of mouth, but are neglectful about the practical aspects of daily Christian living. Conversely, other Christians are careful about their conduct, but fail to witness openly to their friends and neighbours. Each of these types of Christian tends to criticise, or despise, the other. Yet both alike are at fault. Good Christian living is no substitute for witnessing by word of mouth. On the other hand, witnessing by word of mouth is no substitute for good Christian living. God requires both. The believer who omits either one or the other does not stand perfect and complete in all the will of God.

Many other similar instances could be quoted. For example, some believers lay great stress on spiritual gifts, but neglect spiritual fruit. Others lay all their emphasis on spiritual fruit, but display no zeal in seeking spiritual gifts. Paul says in **1 Corinthians 14:1:**

> *Pursue love,* (that is, spiritual fruit) *and desire spiritual gifts...*

In other words, God requires both spiritual gifts and spiritual fruit. Gifts are no substitute for fruit; and fruit is no substitute for gifts.

Again, in presenting the truth of the gospel, there are those who lay all the weight of their preaching on the facts of God's foreknowledge and predestination; while others present only those texts which deal with the free response of man's will. Often these two different lines of approach lead to some kind of doctrinal conflict. Yet each, by itself, is incomplete, and even misleading. The total plan of salvation contains room both for God's predestination on the one hand, and for man's free choice on the other. It is wrong to emphasise either to the exclusion of the other.

This same general principle applies also to the baptism in the Holy Spirit. For those believers who sincerely desire to enter into all the fulness of victorious and fruitful Christian living, the baptism in the Holy Spirit is the greatest single help that God has provided. But even so, it is no substitute for any of the other main parts of Christian experience, or duty.

For example, the baptism in the Spirit is no substitute for regular personal Bible study; or for a daily life of consecration and self denial; or for faithful participation in the activities of a vigorous and spiritual local church.

A believer who is faithful in all these other aspects of the Christian life, but who has not received the baptism in the Holy Spirit, will probably prove a much more effective Christian than one who has received the baptism in the Spirit, but who neglects these other aspects of the Christian life. On the other hand, if the believer who is already faithful in these other duties, goes on to receive the baptism in the Holy Spirit, he will immediately find that the benefits and the effectiveness of all his other activities will be wonderfully enriched and increased by this new experience.

We may illustrate this point by the example of two men - Mr A and Mr B - each of whom has the task of watering a garden. Mr A has the advantage of using a hose, attached directly to a tap. Mr B has only a watering can, which he must fill from the tap, and then carry backwards and forwards to each place in the garden where water is needed. Obviously Mr A starts with a great advantage. He needs only to carry the nozzle of the hose in his hand, and then direct the water wherever he wishes. Mr B has the labour of carrying the can to and fro the whole time.

Let us suppose, however, that Mr B has a great superiority of character over Mr A. Mr A is by nature lazy, erratic, unreliable. Sometimes he forgets to water the garden altogether; at other times he waters some areas, but omits those which need watering most urgently. At other times he takes no care to direct the hose correctly, with the result that he wastes large quantities of water in places where it is not needed and can do no good.

On the other hand, Mr B is active, diligent, and reliable. He never forgets to water the garden at any time; he never passes by any areas that urgently need water; he never wastes any of the water from his can, but carefully directs each drop where it will do the utmost good.

What will be the result? Obviously Mr B will have a much more fruitful and attractive garden than Mr A. However, it would be quite wrong to deduce from this that, as a means of watering a garden, a watering can is superior to a hose.

The superiority is not that of the watering can over the hose, but that of Mr B's whole character over Mr A's. This is proved by the fact that if Mr B now changes over from the watering can to the hose, and continues as faithful with the hose as he was previously with the can, the results which he will be able to achieve with the hose will far excel those which he previously achieved with the can. Furthermore, he will save himself a great deal of time and effort, which he will be free to devote to other useful purposes.

Let us now apply this little parable to the experience of the baptism in the Spirit. Mr A, with the hose, represents the believer who has received the baptism in the Spirit, but who is lazy, erratic, and unreliable in other main aspects of Christian duty. Mr B, with the watering can, represents the believer who has not received the baptism in the Spirit, but who is active, diligent, and reliable in other areas of Christian duty.

In all probability, Mr B will prove to be a more fruitful and effective Christian than Mr A. However, it would be quite illogical to conclude from this that there is anything amiss with the baptism in the Spirit as Mr A received it. The fault lies not in the experience itself, but in the failure of Mr A to make the right use of it thereafter in his daily life.

Furthermore, although Mr B's general faithfulness of character already makes him in a measure an effective and fruitful Christian, the same faithfulness, when enriched and empowered by the baptism in the Spirit, would enable him to become even more fruitful and effective than he was previously.

However much, therefore, we may admire Mr B's faithfulness, we still cannot deny that he is foolish not to seek and to receive the baptism in the Spirit. He is foolish not to exchange the watering can for the hose.

We see, then, that the baptism in the Holy Spirit is not just an unusual and isolated phenomenon, which can be detached from the whole context of Christian experience and duty as revealed in the New Testament. On the contrary, the baptism in the Spirit will only produce the benefits and blessings which God intends, when it is joined together, in active Christian service, with all the other main parts of God's total provision for the believer. Isolated from the rest of Christian life and service, it loses its true signficance, and fails to achieve its true purpose.

In fact, to seek the baptism in the Spirit without sincerely purposing to use the power thus received in scriptural service for Christ can be extremely dangerous.

A New Realm Of Spiritual Conflict

One main reason for this is that the baptism in the Spirit does not merely lead into a realm of new spiritual blessing; it leads also into a realm of new spiritual conflict. As a logical consequence, increased power from God will always bring with it increased opposition from Satan.

The Christian who makes sensible, scriptural use of the power received through the baptism in the Spirit will be in a position to meet and overcome the increased opposition of Satan. On the other hand, the Christian who receives the baptism in the Spirit, but neglects the other aspects of Christian duty, will find himself in an exceedingly dangerous position. He will discover that the baptism in the Spirit has opened up his spiritual nature to entirely new forms of Satanic attack or oppression; but he will be without the God-appointed means to discern the true nature of Satan's attack, or to defend himself against it.

Quite often, such a Christian will find his mind invaded by strange moods of doubt, or fear, or depression; or he will be exposed to forms of moral or spiritual temptation which he never experienced before receiving the baptism in the Spirit. Unless he is forewarned and forearmed to meet those new forms of Satanic attack, he may easily succumb to the wiles and onslaughts of the enemy, and fall back to a lower spiritual level than he was on before he entered this new realm of conflict.

The life of Jesus provides a graphic example of this truth. At His baptism in the Jordan, the Holy Spirit descended on Him in the form of a dove, and remained on Him. Immediately after this, the Holy Spirit led Him to a direct personal encounter with Satan. This is recorded in **Luke 4:1-2:**

> *Then Jesus, being filled with the Holy Spirit, returned from the Jordan and was led by the Spirit into the wilderness,*
> *being tempted for forty days by the devil.*

Luke emphasises at this point that Jesus was now *filled with the Holy Spirit.* This was the very cause why, at this stage in His ministry, He was thrust into direct conflict with the devil.

In the next eleven verses Luke goes on to record how Jesus met and overcame the three main, successive temptations of Satan. Then in **Luke 4:14,** he continues:

> *Then Jesus returned in the power of the Spirit to Galilee...*

Notice the new phrase which Luke uses here: *in the power of the Spirit.* When Jesus went into the wilderness, he was already *filled with the Spirit;* but when he came out of the wilderness again, he came *in the power of the Spirit.* This represents a higher level of spiritual experience. The full power of the Holy Spirit was now freely at his disposal for use in His God-appointed ministry. How had He entered into this higher level of experience? By meeting and overcoming Satan face to face.

Furthermore, in overcoming Satan, Jesus used one weapon, and only one. That was the weapon described by Paul in **Ephesians 6:17:** 'the sword of the Spirit which is the Word of God.' Each time that Satan tempted Him, Jesus began His answer with the phrase, *'It is written.'* That is, He encountered Satan with the direct quotation of God's written Word. Against this weapon Satan has no defence.

This part of the experience of Jesus is a pattern for all those who will follow Him into the Spirit-filled life and ministry. In the life of every believer, it is God's unchanging purpose that the fulness of the Holy Spirit should be joined together with the regular, effective use of God's written Word. Only by this means can the believer expect to come victorious through the new spiritual conflicts which the baptism in the Holy Spirit will inevitably bring upon him.

Since the Word of God is called *the sword of the Spirit,* it follows that the believer who does not use God's Word automatically deprives the Holy Spirit of the main weapon which He desires to use on the believer's behalf. As an inevitable result, the believer's whole spiritual protection becomes inadequate. On the other hand, the believer who at this stage faithfully studies and applies God's Word, will find that this weapon is now being wielded on his behalf by a power and a wisdom far greater than his own - that is, the power and wisdom of the Holy Spirit Himself.

SECTION A: THE SPIRIT-FILLED BELIEVER

Chapter 2

POWER AND GLORY

We have seen that the Holy Spirit is not a dictator. He will not do for us - or through us - more than we allow Him to. There are three main areas to which we may apply this principle: the life of the individual believer; the worship and service of a congregation as a whole; the ministry of a preacher of the gospel.

In the section that now follows, we shall consider the first of these areas. What are the main results that the baptism in the Holy Spirit is intended to produce in the life of each individual Christian? We shall look at eight specific results.

Power To Witness

Christ Himself points to the first of these results in two passages where He gives final words of direction to His disciples, before His ascension into heaven.

In **Luke 24:49,** He says:

> *"Behold, I send the Promise of My Father upon you; but tarry in the city of Jerusalem until you are endued with power from on high."*

Again in **Acts 1:8:**

> *"But you shall receive power when the Holy Spirit has come upon you; and you shall be witnesses to Me in Jerusalem, and in all Judea and Samaria, and to the end of the earth."*

In these passages, Jesus gives His outline plan for the spread of the gospel in the present age. It is extremely simple. It contains three successive stages. First, each believer is to be personally empowered by the Holy Spirit; second, each believer, thus empowered by the Spirit, is by his personal testimony to win others to Christ; third, these others are in their turn to be empowered by the Spirit to win yet others. In this way the testimony of Christ is to be extended outward from Jerusalem in ever-widening circles of power until it has reached the end of the earth - that is, until it has reached all nations and every creature.

This plan is both simple and practical. Whenever it is applied, it will always work. It would make possible the evangelisation of the entire world in any century in which the church would put the plan to work. There is no other alternative plan which can accomplish the same result.

In these passages in which Jesus speaks of the baptism in the Holy Spirit, the key word is 'power.' The Greek word is 'dunamis,' from which we get such English words as'dynamo,' 'dynamic,' 'dynamite.' The impression produced by these English derivative words is essentially that of a 'forceful, explosive impact.'

In this respect, the New Testament observes a very careful, logical distinction between the primary results of the new birth, and the primary results of the baptism in the Holy Spirit.

The primary concept associated with the new birth is authority. For instance, in **John 1:12** we read:

> But as many as received Him (Christ), to them He gave the right to become children of God...

This passage describes the new birth, for in the next verse we are told that these people who received Christ *were born of God*. The Greek word here translated *the right* is 'exousia.' 'Exousia' denotes a being, or a nature, which is derived from some external source. In other words, the person who receives Christ as Saviour receives, in Christ, the being, or nature, of God Himself. The receiving of this new life, or nature, from God produces within the believer the new birth.

The English word most commonly used to translate this Greek word 'exousia' is 'authority.' This is the distinctive mark of the born again child of God. He is no longer a slave of sin and of Satan. He is a son of God. As such, he possesses a new authority. He no longer succumbs to temptation, or opposition. He meets and overcomes these things by virtue of the new life within him. He is an overcomer. He has 'authority.'

However, 'authority' is not at all the same as 'power.' The first disciples already had this authority from the time of Christ's resurrection onwards. They were already 'sons of God.' They were able to lead godly, overcoming lives. They were no longer the slaves of sin. However, during the period from the resurrection to the day of Pentecost, these first disciples made very little positive impact upon the great majority of the inhabitants of Jerusalem. As a whole, during this period, the city of Jerusalem was very little changed, or affected, by the fact of Christ's resurrection.

All this was abruptly and dramatically changed, however, by the descent of the Holy Spirit on the day of Pentecost. As soon as the 120 believers in the upper room were baptised in the Holy Spirit, the whole of Jerusalem immediately felt the impact. Within an hour or two a crowd of many thousands had gathered, and before the day closed, three thousand Christ-rejecting unbelievers had been gloriously converted, baptised, and added to the church.

What produced these dramatic results? The adding of 'power' to 'authority.' Before the day of Pentecost the disciples already had 'authority.' After Pentecost they had 'authority' plus 'power' - they had the 'power' that was needed to make their 'authority' fully effective.

The evidence and outworking of this new, supernatural power are conspicuous in the ensuing chapters of the book of Acts.

In **Acts 4:31,** we read:

...and they were all filled with the Holy Spirit, and they spoke the Word of God with boldness.

In **Acts 4:33:**

And with great power the apostles gave witness to the resurrection of the Lord Jesus.

In **Acts 5:28,** the High Priest complains to the apostles:

"...And look, you have filled Jerusalem with your doctrine..."

143

The same city-shaking impact continued to make itself felt thereafter in every place where the early Christians presented the testimony of the risen Christ in the power of the Holy Spirit.

For instance, we read in **Acts 8:8,** concerning Samaria:

And there was great joy in that city.

Concerning the city of Antioch in Pisidia we read, in **Acts 13:44:**

And the next Sabbath almost the whole city came together to hear the Word of God.

In **Acts 16:20,** in the city of Philippi, the opponents of the gospel complained concerning Paul and Silas:

"These men, being Jews, exceedingly trouble our city..."

In **Acts 17:6,** in Thessalonica, the opponents of the gospel said of Paul and Silas:

"These who have turned the world upside down have come here too."

In **Acts 19:29,** we read that, as a result of the opposition to Paul's preaching in Ephesus:

...the whole city was filled with confusion.

There was one common feature which marked the advent of these early Christian witnesses in every place: a mighty spiritual impact upon the whole community. In some places there was a revival; in some there was a riot; quite often there were both together. But there were two things that could not survive this impact: ignorance, and indifference.

Today, in many places, the conduct and experience of professing Christians are very different. This applies even to many groups of Christians who have a genuine experience of the new birth. They meet regularly in a church building for worship; they lead decent, respectable lives; they cause no trouble; they provoke no riots; they arouse no opposition. But alas! they make no impact. In the community all round them, ignorance and indifference concerning spiritual things prevail, unchanged and unchallenged.

144

The vast majority of their neighbours neither know nor care what these Christians believe, or why they attend church.

What is lacking? The answer lies in one word: 'power.' The explosive dynamite of the Holy Spirit has been left out of these Christians' lives. And nothing else can take its place.

The Christian Church as a whole needs to face up to the challenge of Paul in **1 Corinthians 4:20:**

For the kingdom of God is not in word but in power.

Once again, the Greek word which Paul here uses is *dunamis* - dynamite - explosive power. It is not a question merely of words which we speak, but of the power which makes our words effective. The key to this spiritual power is the baptism in the Holy Spirit. For this, there is no substitute.

We see, then, that, according to the New Testament, the primary result of the baptism in the Holy Spirit is a supernatural enduement with power from on high to become an effective witness for Christ.

Glorification Of Christ

The second main result of the baptism in the Holy Spirit is indicated by the words of Peter on the day of Pentecost, as recorded in **Acts 2:33:**

Therefore being exalted to the right hand of God, and having received from the Father the promise of the Holy Spirit, He (Christ) *poured out this which you now see and hear.*

The baptism in the Holy Spirit, which Peter and the other disciples had just received, constituted for each of them direct, personal evidence and assurance that their risen Lord was now both exalted and glorified at the Father's right hand.

Ten days earlier, a little group of them had stood on the Mount of Olives and watched Jesus taken up from them out of their sight. **Acts 1:9** states:

...and a cloud received Him out of their sight.

That was the last contact that the disciples had with Jesus through their physical senses. Then ten days later, on the day of Pentecost, the coming of the Holy Spirit gave to each one of the disciples in the upper room a new, direct and personal contact with Christ. Each one of them knew now, with a fresh assurance, that their Saviour, whom the world had despised, rejected and crucified, was henceforth and forever exalted and glorified at the right hand of the Father in heaven.

Only from the Father's presence could Jesus have received this wonderful gift of the Holy Spirit which He, in turn, imparted to His waiting disciples. Receiving this gift gave them total assurance that Jesus was actually in the glory of the Father's presence, invested with authority and power over the entire universe.

There are many Scriptures which emphasise the supreme exaltation of Jesus Christ.

For example, in **Ephesians 1:20-23,** we read that:

> *..He* (God) *raised Him from the dead and seated Him at His right hand in the heavenly places,*
> *far above all principality and power and might and dominion, and every name that is named, not only in this age but also in that which is to come.*
> *And He put all things under His feet, and gave Him to be head over all things to the church,*
> *which is His body, the fullness of Him who fills all in all.*

Again, in **Philippians 2:9:**

> *Therefore God also has highly exalted Him and given Him the name which is above every name...*

In **Hebrews 1:3-4,** we read that:

> *...when He had by Himself purged our sins,* (He) *sat down at the right hand of the Majesty on high,*
> *having become so much better than the angels, as He has by inheritance obtained a more excellent name than they.*

In **1 Peter 3:22,** the apostle says of Christ after His resurrection:

> *...who has gone into heaven and is at the right hand of God, angels and authorities and powers having been made subject to Him.*

Through these and other Scriptures every believer understands, by faith, that Jesus Christ is not merely risen from the dead; He is also ascended and glorified at the Father's right hand. However, the believer who receives the baptism in the Holy Spirit receives with it a new kind of direct, personal evidence and assurance of Christ's exaltation in power and glory at the Father's throne.

Often, when a loved one leaves us on a journey to some new destination, we urge him: 'Be sure and send us a letter to let us know that you have arrived safely.' Then, when the letter arrives, in the loved one's own handwriting, and postmarked with the name of the city of destination, we know, with full assurance, that he is in the very place of which he told us before leaving.

So it is with the baptism in the Holy Spirit. For the disciples on the day of Pentecost - and for every individual believer thereafter who receives the same experience - it is like a personal letter received direct from Christ. The postmark on the letter is 'Glory,' and the message reads: 'I am here, just as I said, at the seat of all authority and power.'

I am reminded in this connection of a conversation that I once had, while serving as principal of a College in East Africa, with a minister of one of the older denominations. This minister was questioning me about my personal experience of receiving the baptism in the Holy Spirit. He designated my form of experience by the title 'Pentecostalism,' and he obviously regarded the whole thing with some suspicion, as the product of some new and eccentric religious sect.

'Now let me see,' he said. 'That started in America, I believe. It comes from the United States, doesn't it?'

'Oh, no!' I replied. 'You're quite wrong about that! This thing started in Jerusalem, and it comes from heaven!'

So it is with every believer who has received the baptism in the Holy Spirit as the first disciples received it on the day of Pentecost. This experience gives him a new, direct contact in two directions: first, with the glorified Christ at the Father's right hand in heaven; second, with the New Testament Church as it came into being in the city of

Jerusalem, and as it is thereafter pictured in the book of Acts.

The baptism in the Holy Spirit gives a new meaning, a new reality, a new assurance, both concerning the exaltation of Christ, and concerning the life and activity of the New Testament Church. Things that before were historical or doctrinal facts, accepted by bare faith, become, for each Spirit-filled believer, thrilling, pulsating realities in his own experience.

This is in line with the statement in **John 7:39,** that, in the days of Christ's earthly ministry, *the Holy Spirit was not yet given, because Jesus was not yet glorified.*

We have already seen earlier that the Holy Spirit could not be given to the Church before Christ was glorified with the Father in heaven. Only the glorified Christ Himself was worthy to exercise the privilege, bestowed by the Father, of giving this wonderful gift. Therefore, the fact that this gift was bestowed upon the disciples on the day of Pentecost was in itself evidence that Christ had been glorified.

Invariably, throughout the New Testament, we find the most perfect harmony and cooperation between the three Persons of the triune Godhead. When Jesus Christ, the second Person of the Godhead, came to earth, He came as the personal, authoritative representative of God the Father. He never sought any kind of honour or glory for Himself. Both His words and His works - His wisdom and His miracles - He invariably ascribed not to Himself, but to His Father, dwelling and working in Him.

Likewise, when in due course Jesus finished His earthly ministry, and returned to the Father in heaven, He in turn sent the Holy Spirit as His personal gift and His personal representative to His Church. The Holy Spirit coming thus as the representative of the second person, the Son of God, never seeks His own glory. His whole ministry on earth and in the Church is always directed to uplifting, magnifying, and glorifying the One whom He represents - that is, Christ.

Jesus Himself spoke of this aspect of the Spirit's ministry in **John 16:14-15:**

148

"He will glorify Me, for He will take of what is Mine and declare it to you.
"All things that the Father has are Mine. Therefore I said that he will take of Mine and declare it to you."

Here we see the relationship between the three Persons of the Godhead very clearly unfolded. The Father bestows all His authority, power and glory upon the Son; the Son in turn appoints the Holy Spirit as His representative, to reveal and interpret to the Church all that He has received from the Father.

It is most important to realise that the Holy Spirit is just as much a Person as the Father and the Son; and therefore that Christ, during the present dispensation, has one, and only one, personal and authoritative representative in the Church and on earth. That representative is none other than the Holy Spirit Himself.

This revelation of the Holy Spirit's ministry provides a simple way to test anything that claims to be inspired by the Spirit. Does it glorify Christ? If the answer is not a clear 'yes,' we have every right to question whether we are dealing with a genuine operation or manifestation of the Holy Spirit.

We find, then, a kind of divine jealousy between Christ and the Holy Spirit. On the one hand, the Holy Spirit is jealous of any trend or teaching that detracts from the honour of Christ as Head over the Church. On the other hand, Christ refuses to lend His authority to any ministry or movement that does not recognise the unique position of the Holy Spirit as His representative within the Church.

The glory of Christ and the ministry of the Holy Spirit are inseparably linked together.

Chapter 3

ON THE SUPERNATURAL PLANE

In this chapter we shall continue to study the results which the baptism in the Holy Spirit is intended by God to produce in the life of each individual believer.

A Gateway To The Supernatural

For a third main result of this experience we may turn to the words of **Hebrews 6:4-5,** which speak of believers who

> ...have become partakers of the Holy Spirit,
> and have tasted the good word of God and the powers
> of the age to come...

These words indicate that those who have been made partakers of the Holy Spirit have, as a result of that experience, tasted *the powers of the age to come.* The baptism in the Holy Spirit gives to the believer a foretaste of an altogether new kind of power - a supernatural power that belongs, in its fulness, to the next age.

For this reason, in **Ephesians 1:13-14,** Paul describes the seal of the Holy Spirit as *the guarantee of our inheritance:*

> In Him you also trusted, after you heard the word of
> truth, the gospel of your salvation; in whom also,
> having believed, you were sealed with the Holy Spirit
> of promise,
> who is the guarantee of our inheritance until the
> redemption of the purchased possession, to the praise
> of His glory.

An alternative translation for *guarantee* is 'down payment.' The Greek word - which is borrowed from Hebrew - is 'arrabon.' This is a very interesting word, which I have encountered - with slight variations - in four different languages: Hebrew, Greek, Arabic and Swahili.

Its meaning was brought home to me in a very vivid way, many years ago in Jerusalem. My first wife, Lydia, and I had moved with our children to a new home, for which we needed to purchase about 20 yards of curtain material. We went to the appropriate section of the Old City and found some suitable material, for which - after some bargaining - we agreed to pay the equivalent of $4 per yard, making a total of $80. I gave the storekeeper a down payment of $20 (called in Arabic an 'arbon'), and promised to come back within a week with the balance of $60.

I reminded the storekeeper that I now regarded the material as already my property. As such, he must set it on one side until I returned, and he had no right even to offer it to any other purchaser.

In the same way, the Lord gives us - through His Holy Spirit - a 'down payment' of heavenly power and glory - a foretaste of the next age. This down payment sets us aside as already His purchased property, not even to be offered to any other purchaser. It is His guarantee, too, that at the appointed time He will return with the balance of payment and take us to His home, to be with Him for ever. That is why Paul calls it *the guarantee of our inheritance **until the redemption of the purchased possession.***

Another beautiful illustration of what we receive through the baptism in the Holy Spirit is contained in the story of the healing of Naaman, the Syrian leper, recorded in **2 Kings 5**. As a result of his miraculous healing, Naaman came to acknowledge that the Lord, Jehovah, the God of Israel, was the only true God. He knew, however, that he would shortly have to return to an unclean, heathen land, and be associated with the idolatrous ceremonies of a heathen temple. With this in mind, we read - in **2 Kings 5:17** - that Naaman had one special request to make before leaving the land of Israel:

> So Naaman said, "Then, if not, please let you servant be given two mule-loads of earth; for your servant

*will no longer offer either burnt offering or sacrifice
to other gods, but to the Lord."*

Why did Naaman desire to carry home this portion of
earth from the land of Israel? He had realised the holiness
of the Lord, and, in contrast, the uncleanness of his own
land and people. He was determined, therefore, never again
to offer worship from unclean earth.

The holiness of the Lord demanded that Naaman should
stand and worship Him only on earth from the Lord's own
land. Since Naaman could not remain permanently in the
land of Israel, he determined to carry a portion of Israel's
earth home with him to his own land, and to make there
from that earth his own special place of worship.

So it is with the Spirit-baptised believer. He gains a new
understanding of the words of Jesus in **John 4:24:**

*"God is Spirit, and those who worship Him must
worship in spirit and truth."*

Such a believer can no longer be satisfied with the mere
forms and ceremonies of man-made worship. He has been
in the heavenly land; he has had a glimpse of its glories,
and of the holiness of God. He has brought back a portion
of that sacred soil with him. No matter where circumstances
may take him, he worships now not on an unclean land,
but on holy ground. He worships in Spirit - that is, in the
Holy Spirit - and in truth.

What is true in the worship of the Spirit-filled believer,
is equally true in every other aspect of his experience.
Through the baptism in the Spirit he has entered into a new
kind of supernatural life. The supernatural has become
natural.

If we study the New Testament with an open mind, we
are compelled to acknowledge that the whole life and experience of the early Christians was permeated in every part
by the supernatural. Supernatural experiences were not
something incidental, or additional; they were an integral
part of their whole lives as Christians. Their praying was
supernatural; their preaching was supernatural; they were
supernaturally guided, supernaturally empowered, supernaturally transported, supernaturally protected.

Remove the supernatural from the book of Acts, and you are left with something that has no meaning or coherence. From the descent of the Holy Spirit in **Acts 2,** and onwards, it is impossible to find a single chapter in which the record of the supernatural does not play an essential part.

In the account of Paul's ministry in Ephesus, in **Acts 19:11,** we find a most arresting and thought-provoking expression:

> *Now God worked unusual miracles by the hands of Paul.*

Consider the implications of that phrase *unusual miracles.* The Greek could be translated, somewhat freely, 'miracles of a kind that do not happen every day.' Miracles were an everyday occurrence in the early church. Normally they would have caused no special surprise, or comment. But the miracles granted here in Ephesus through the ministry of Paul were such that even the early church found them worthy of special record.

In how many churches today would we find occasion to use the phrase - 'miracles of a kind that do not happen every day'? In how many churches today do miracles ever happen - let alone, happen every day?

The truth is that, where we do not see and experience the supernatural, we have no right to speak of New Testament Christianity. These two things - the supernatural, and New Testament Christianity - are inseparably interwoven.

Without the supernatural, we may have New Testament doctrine, but it is bare doctrine, not experience. Such doctrine, divorced from supernatural experience, is of the kind described by Paul in **2 Corinthians 3:6:**

> *...for the letter kills, but the Spirit gives life.*

It is the Holy Spirit, and He alone, who can give life to the letter of New Testament doctrine, and can make that doctrine a living, personal, supernatural way of life for each believer. One main purpose of the baptism in the Holy Spirit is to do just this.

Spirit-Empowered Prayer

A fourth main purpose of the baptism in the Holy Spirit concerns the prayer life of the believer. The key text for this is found in **Romans 8:26-27:**

> *Likewise the Spirit also helps in our weaknesses. For we do not know what we should pray for as we ought, but the Spirit Himself makes intercession for us with groanings which cannot be uttered.*
> *Now He who searches the hearts knows what the mind of the Spirit is, because He makes intercession for the saints according to the will of God.*

Paul mentions one form of weakness which is common to all believers in their own natural condition and apart from the Holy Spirit. This is not a weakness in the sense of a disease, or a bodily infirmity. It is defined by Paul in the words: *for we do not know what we should pray for as we ought.* This weakness consists in not knowing how to pray aright, in being unable to pray in accordance with God's will.

The only one to whom we can turn for help in this weakness is the Holy Spirit, for Paul says:

> *...the Spirit also helps in our weaknesses...the Spirit Himself make intercession for us...because He makes intercession for the saints according to the will of God.*

Paul here speaks of the Spirit as a Person who indwells the believer, and who makes the believer a vessel, or a channel, through which He, the Spirit Himself, offers prayer and intercession.

This is prayer of a kind which is far above the level of the believer's own natural understanding, or ability. In this kind of prayer the believer does not rely on his feelings or his understanding; but he yields his body to the Holy Spirit as a temple in which the Spirit Himself conducts prayer, and he yields his members as instruments which the Spirit controls for purposes of supernatural intercession.

As we study the teaching of the New Testament concerning prayer, we find that it sets a standard to which the believer can never attain in his own natural strength or understanding. In this way, God deliberately shuts the believer up in a place where he is obliged either to fall below the divine standard, or else to depend upon the supernatural assistance of the indwelling Spirit.

For example, Paul says in **Ephesians 6:18:**

...praying always with all prayer and supplication in the Spirit...

And again, in **1 Thessalonians 5:17-19:**

...pray without ceasing...Do not quench the Spirit.

Such is the natural infirmity of the human flesh and mind, that no person, in his own unaided strength or understanding, can fulfil these commandments. No person can *pray always,* or *pray without ceasing.* But that which is impossible in the natural is made possible by the indwelling, supernatural presence of the Holy Spirit. For this reason, in both these passages, Paul is careful to emphasise the believer's dependence upon the Holy Spirit. He says: *praying always...in the Spirit;* and again *pray without ceasing...Do not quench the Spirit.*

The Holy Spirit indwelling the believer in the New Testament corresponds to the fire supernaturally kindled upon the altar of the tabernacle in the Old Testament. Concerning this fire the Lord ordained in **Leviticus 6:13:**

A perpetual fire shall burn on the altar; it shall never go out.

The corresponding New Testament ordinance is contained in the words of Paul: *pray without ceasing...Do not quench the Spirit.* Where the Spirit-baptised believer yields full contol to the Spirit within, and does not by carelessness, or carnality, quench the Spirit's fire, there burns within the temple of that believer's body a fire of supernatural prayer and worship, which never goes out, day or night. Few people realise the limitless potentialities of Holy Spirit prayer within the temple of a believer's yielded body.

Some years ago, when I conducted regular street meetings in the city of London, England, a young woman of Catholic background from Ireland came under the sound of the gospel, and was saved and baptised in the Holy Spirit. She was working at that time as a maid in a London hotel, and she shared a bedroom there with another young woman of her own age and background. One day this other woman came to her and said: 'Tell me, what is that strange language you speak to yourself every night in bed, after you seem to have gone to sleep?'

'I can't tell you that,' the first young woman answered, 'because I never even knew that I was speaking any language.'

In this way, she learned to her surprise that every night, after she had gone to sleep, without the conscious exercise of her own faculties, she was speaking with other tongues, as the Holy Spirit gave her utterance.

So it is, to be filled with, and yielded to, the Holy Spirit. When we come to the end of our own natural strength and understanding, the Holy Spirit can take over our faculties and conduct His own worship and prayer through us.

This is the picture given of the bride of Christ in the **Song of Solomon 5:2:**

> *I sleep, but my heart is awake...*

The bride may sleep; she may be physically and mentally exhausted. But in the innermost depths of her being there dwells one who never slumbers or sleeps - the Holy Spirit Himself. Even through the hours of darkness, there burns upon the altar of her heart a fire that never goes out - a fire of worship and prayer that is the life of the Holy Spirit within.

This is the Bible pattern for the prayer life of the Church in this present age. But such a life of prayer is possible only through the supernatural, indwelling presence of the Holy Spirit Himself.

Revelation Of The Scriptures

A fifth great purpose of the baptism in the Holy Spirit is that the Spirit may become our guide and teacher in relation to the Scriptures.

Christ promises this to His disciples in two passages in John's Gospel.

In **John 14:26,** He says:

> *"But the Helper, the Holy Spirit, whom the Father*

will send in My name, He will teach you all things,
and bring to your remembrance all things that I said
to you."

During the earthly ministry of Jesus there was much
that He taught His disciples, especially concerning His death
and resurrection, which the disciples at that time were
unable either to understand or to remember.

However, Jesus assured them that after the Holy Spirit
came to dwell in them, He would become their personal
teacher, and would enable them both to remember and to
understand correctly all that Jesus had taught them during
His earthly ministry. Nor would the Holy Spirit confine
Himself only to interpreting the teaching of Jesus while on
earth; He would also lead the disciples into a full understanding of God's whole revelation to man.

In **John 16:13** Jesus returns to this theme:

"However, when He, the Spirit of truth, has come,
He will guide you into all truth (more literally, into
all the truth); *for He will not speak on His own*
authority, but whatever he hears He will speak..."

Here the phrase *all the truth* may be interpreted by reference
to the words of Jesus in **John 17:17:** *"Your word is truth."*

Jesus promises His disciples that the Holy Spirit will
lead them into a correct understanding of the entire revelation of God to man through the Scriptures. This includes
the Old Testament Scriptures, the teaching of Jesus during
His earthly ministry, and also the further revelation of truth
given to the Church after Pentecost through Paul and others
of the apostles.

The Holy Spirit is given to the Church to become the
revelator, interpreter and teacher of the whole compass of
divine revelation in the Scriptures.

The fulfilment of Christ's promise that the Holy Spirit
would interpret the Scriptures for the disciples is dramatically illustrated in the events of the day of Pentecost. As
soon as the Holy Spirit was poured out upon the disciples
and they began to speak with other tongues, the question
was raised: "Whatever could this mean?"

In **Acts 2:16-17**, Peter answered:

"But this is what was spoken by the prophet Joel:
'And it shall come to pass in the last days, says God,
That I will pour out of My Spirit on all flesh...'"

Peter then goes on, without a moment's hesitation, to quote and interpret a prophecy concerning the last days given in the second chapter of the prophet Joel. In the sermon which follows, almost half of what Peter says is direct quotation from the Old Testament Scriptures; and the teaching of these Scriptures is applied in a most clear and forceful way to the events of Christ's death and resurrection and of the Holy Spirit's outpouring.

It is difficult to imagine any greater contrast between the exposition of the Old Testament Scriptures here given by Peter, and the lack of understanding concerning the same Scriptures displayed by Peter and all the other disciples during the earthly ministry of Jesus and up to the day of Pentecost.

It would appear that this total change in the disciples' understanding of the Scriptures was not a gradual process, but was produced instantaneously by the coming of the Holy Spirit. As soon as the Holy Spirit came to indwell them their understanding of the Scriptures was supernaturally illuminated. Their previous doubts and confusion were immediately replaced by clear understanding and forceful application.

This same dramatic transformation continues to be a distinctive mark of Spirit-filled believers from the day of Pentecost onwards.

For example, Saul of Tarsus had been trained in the knowledge of the Old Testament Scriptures by Gamaliel, the most famous teacher of his day. Yet in his early years, he had no light or understanding on their correct application. It was only after Ananias in Damascus laid hands on Saul, and prayed that he might be filled with the Holy Spirit, that the scales fell from his eyes and he was able to understand and apply those Scriptures.

After this experience, we read in **Acts 9:20:**

Immediately he preached the Christ in the synagogues,
that He is the Son of God.

158

Notice that word *immediately*. There was not a slow, gradual struggle for understanding, but rather an instant illumination. The moment that the Holy Spirit came in, He cast an altogether new light upon Scriptures which Saul had known for many years, but had never known how to apply or to interpret.

What the Holy Spirit did for Peter, and for Saul, and for the New Testament Christians as a whole, He is still willing and able to do for all Christians today. But first each believer must, through the baptism in the Holy Spirit, personally receive this wonderful indwelling guide, teacher, and expositor.

Chapter 4

CONTINUAL GUIDANCE AND OVERFLOWING LIFE

In this chapter we shall consider two further ministries of the Holy Spirit in the life of the believer: daily guidance in the path of God's will; and the impartation of life and health to the believer's physical body.

Daily Guidance

The first of these ministries is described by Paul in **Romans 8:14:**

For as many as are led by the Spirit of God, these are the sons of God.

It is important to see that Paul here uses a continuing present tense: *as many as are being* (regularly) *led by the Spirit of God...* He is not talking about a few isolated experiences, but about an ongoing way of life.

Many professing Christians, even among those who have been truly born again, do not attach sufficient importance to these words of Paul. They tend to place their whole emphasis on certain one-time experiences, such as the new birth or the baptism in the Holy Spirit, on which they base their claim to be considered Christians. It is certainly important to emphasise these decisive experiences, but not to the point where no mention is made of the need to walk daily in the grace of God.

In order to become a true Christian, a person must be born again of the Spirit of God. In order to become an effective witness for Christ, a person must be baptised in the Holy Spirit. But the work of the Holy Spirit should never end there. In order to live daily as a Christian, a person must be led by the Spirit.

The new birth transforms sinners into children of God. But it requires the continual leading of the Holy Spirit to make children into mature sons.

In **Romans 8:14,** Paul takes for granted the two preliminary experiences of being born of the Holy Spirit and baptised in the Holy Spirit. He points out, however, that the only way to achieve spiritual maturity and success in daily Christian living is to depend upon the Spirit for moment-by-moment direction in every aspect of life. Only this will make it possible for the Holy Spirit to accomplish all the purposes for which He actually came to indwell the believer.

This is in harmony with what Paul says in **Ephesians 2:10:**

For we are His workmanship, created in Christ Jesus for good works, which God prepared beforehand that we should walk in them.

As believers, Paul teaches, we are created anew by God through our faith in Christ. Thereafter, to continue in the Christian life, we do not have to plan our own ways and activities. On the contrary, the same God, who first foreknew us, and then created us anew in Christ, also prepared from before the foundation of the world the good works which it was His will for each one of us to accomplish as Christians.

Therefore, we do not plan our own good works, but we seek to discover, and then to enter into, the good works which God has already planned for us. It is at this point that the guidance of the Holy Spirit becomes essential for each Christian. For it is the Holy Spirit who first reveals, and then leads us into, God's plan for our lives as Christians.

Unfortunately, many Christians today have in effect reversed this process. They first plan their own ways and their own activities; and then they say some kind of perfunctory prayer, asking God to grant His blessing to the ways and activities which they have planned for themselves. However, it is perfectly certain that, in reality, almighty God will never allow His approval or blessing to become a mere rubber stamp superimposed upon plans and activities concerning which His counsel has never really been sincerely sought.

This error is common, not only in the lives of individual Christians, but also in the activities of churches and other Christian organisations, both at home and overseas. In many different spheres of Christian activity, countless hours of labour and vast sums of money are squandered and lost, without any enduring fruit, simply because the counsel of almighty God was never sincerely sought before these various forms of activity were initiated.

In fact, in many Christian circles today, the greatest enemy of true spirituality and fruitfulness is time-consuming, sweat-producing activity, labelled 'Christian' in name, but lacking the divine inbreathing and directing of the Holy Spirit.

The end products of all such activity are described by Paul, in **1 Corinthians 3:12,** as *wood, hay, straw* - all of which will be consumed, without residue or remainder, in the fire of God's final judgment upon His people's works.

In contrast to all this, one of the distinguishing marks of the New Testament church is the direct, continued, supernatural guidance of the Holy Spirit in all its activities. Out of many possible examples of this in the book of Acts, it will be sufficient to consider one very characteristic incident from Paul's second missionary journey, on which he was accompanied by Silas. This is described in **Acts 16:6-10:**

> *Now when they had gone through Phrygia and the region of Galatia, they were forbidden by the Holy Spirit to preach the word in Asia.*
> *After they had come to Mysia, they tried to go into Bithynia, but the Spirit did not permit them.*
> *So passing by Mysia, they came down to Troas.*
> *And a vision appeared to Paul in the night. A man of Macedonia stood and pleaded with him, saying, "Come over to Macedonia and help us."*
> *Now after he had seen the vision, immediately we sought to go to Macedonia, concluding that the Lord had called us to preach the gospel to them.*

In considering this passage, we must bear in mind

that Paul and Silas in their missionary undertaking were fulfilling the direct commission of Jesus to His disciples, given in **Matthew 28:19:**

"Go therefore and make disciples of all the nations..."

And again, in **Mark 16:15:**

"Go into all the world and preach the gospel to every creature."

Notice how all-inclusive this commission is: *all the nations; every creature.*

In fulfilment of this commission, Paul and Silas had been preaching in Phrygia and Galatia - that is, in the central part of what we today call Asia Minor. Their next obvious move would have been into the province of Asia, on the western edge of Asia Minor. However, the record of Acts says: *'they were forbidden by the Holy Spirit to preach the word in Asia.'* As a result, they moved to the north of Asia, into Mysia.

From here, their next obvious move would have been northeast, into Bithynia. However, at this point Acts records: *'they tried to go into Bithynia, but the Spirit did not permit them.'*

In this way, both the obvious doors of evangelisation - into Asia on the one side, and into Bithynia on the other side - were closed to them by the direct, explicit decree of the Holy Spirit.

Doubtless, Paul and Silas began to wonder what God's plan for them could be, or what course they should follow next. But at this point, Paul had a vision in the night of a man of Macedonia saying, *'Come over to Macedonia, and help us.'* Without further question, they immediately realised that God was directing them to Macedonia - in the northern part of Greece, and in the southeastern corner of the continent of Europe proper. In this way, the gospel was for the first time brought over out of Asia into Europe.

As we now look back over nineteen subsequent centuries of church history, we realise the decisive part played by the church in Europe, first in preserving the truth of the gospel, and then in actively disseminating that truth again throughout the rest of the world. We can understand therefore why, in the wisdom and foreknowledge of God, it was of the utmost urgency and importance that the gospel should, thus early, be planted in Europe by Paul himself, the chief apostle of the Gentiles.

However, Paul and Silas themselves knew nothing of the course that history would take in the next nineteen centuries. Therefore, their taking of this epoch-making step into Europe was made possible solely through the supernatural revelation and direction of the Holy Spirit. If they had not been open in this way to the Spirit's guidance, they would have missed God's plan, both for their own lives and also for the whole work of the gospel.

God's supernatural direction of Paul through the Holy Spirit at this point is made all the more remarkable when we consider certain subsequent phases of Paul's missionary activity.

Here, in **Acts 16,** we read that Paul was forbidden by the Holy Spirit to preach the word in the province of Asia, and therefore he journeyed right past Asia and on into Europe. Yet, in **Acts 19,** we read how Paul returned some time later to the city of Ephesus, which was the main city of the province of Asia; and how at this time there developed out of his preaching there one of the greatest and most extensive revivals ever recorded in his whole ministry.

The impact of Paul's ministry in Ephesus at this time is summed up in **Acts 19:10:**

> *And this continued for two years, so that all who dwelt in Asia heard the word of the Lord Jesus, both Jews and Greeks.*

Surely this is worthy of our careful consideration. Earlier, Paul had not been allowed by the Holy Spirit even to enter Asia, or to speak to a single soul there. Now, returning there at God's appointed time and under the Holy Spirit's guidance, Paul witnessed in this same province of Asia such an impact through the preaching of the gospel that every single human soul dwelling in the entire province came to hear the testimony of Christ.

On the basis of these facts, we may venture to form two conclusions. First, if Paul had entered Asia on this first visit, contrary to the Spirit's direction, he would have encountered nothing but frustration and failure. In fact, we can imagine that, in the language of modern missions, Asia would have been described as 'a most difficult field.' Second, by visiting Asia prematurely, before the Spirit led him there, Paul could easily have hindered, or even totally prevented, the subsequent mighty move of God's Spirit which he was privileged to witness on his later visit.

What a lesson there is here for all who seek to preach the gospel or to witness for Christ in any way. In every course of proposed activity, there are two factors of related importance which we must take into account: the first is the place; the second is the time.

In this, the revelation of Scripture anticipates the basic conclusion of the modern scientific theory of relativity: that we can never accurately specify place, unless we also specify time. These two are interrelated, and can never be separated the one from the other.

In other language, this same truth was stated, many centuries ago, by Solomon in **Ecclesiastes 3:1:**

To everything there is a season,
A time for every purpose under heaven...

It is not enough merely to do the right thing, or to have the right purpose. In order to enjoy success and the blessing of God, we must do **the right thing at the right time,** and we must carry out **the right purpose at the right season.** When God says 'Now,' it is vain for man to says 'Later'; and conversely, when God say 'Later,' it is vain for man to say 'Now.'

It is the God-appointed ministry of the Holy Spirit to reveal to the Church not merely the right thing or the right purpose, but also the right time and the right season. Many sincere and well-meaning Christians, who have not learned to make room in their experience for the guidance of the Holy Spirit, encounter continual frustration in their lives simply through seeking to do the right thing at the wrong time, and to carry out the right purpose at the wrong season.

In this connection, in **Isaiah 40:13,** the prophet poses a very searching question:

> *Who has directed the Spirit of the Lord,*
> *Or as His counsellor has taught Him?*

Yet this is just what many sincere and well meaning Christians are doing today: they are seeking to direct the Spirit of the Lord and to act as counsellor to the Holy Spirit. They plan their own activities, conduct their own services, and then tell the Holy Spirit just what, and when, and how, they expect Him to bless. In how many congregations today is there any real room left for the Holy Spirit either to direct, or to intervene?

The result, in the lives of believers, of this wrong attitude toward the Holy Spirit, can be summed up in one word: frustration.

Such believers may have a genuine experience of the new birth, and even of the baptism in the Holy Spirit; they may be perfectly sincere in their profession of faith in Christ. Nevertheless, in their daily lives they lack either victory or fruitfulness, because they have overlooked this one cardinal rule of Christian living: *'For as many as are led by the Spirit of God, these are sons of God.'*

Life For The Whole Person

The continual guidance of God in the life of the believer opens the way for yet another provision of His Spirit: overflowing life for his whole personality. The relationship between God's guidance and this all-sufficient life is beautifully described in **Isaiah 58:11:**

> *The Lord will guide you continually,*
> *And satisfy your soul in drought,*
> *And strengthen your bones;*
> *You shall be like a watered garden,*
> *And like a spring of water, whose waters do not fail.*

Isaiah depicts a person so continually guided by God that he has within him a spring of life which overflows throughout his whole personality, refreshing and renewing both his soul and his body.

In the New Testament Paul traces this overflowing life to its source: the Holy Spirit indwelling the believer.

In **Romans 1:4** he says that Jesus Christ was:

> ...*declared to be the Son of God with power, according to the Spirit of holiness, by the resurrection from the dead...*

It was *the Spirit of holiness* - a Hebraic expression for 'the Holy Spirit' - who raised up the dead body of Jesus from the grave, thus vindicating His claim to be the Son of God.

In **Romans 8:11** Paul reveals that the Holy Spirit will perform the same ministry for every believer whom He indwells:

> *But if the Spirit of Him who raised Jesus from the dead dwells in you, He who raised Christ from the dead will also give life to your mortal bodies through His Spirit who dwells in you.*

This ministry of the Holy Spirit will receive its full and final outworking at the first resurrection, when He will raise up the righteous dead with the same kind of immortal body that Jesus already has. Paul reaffirms this in **2 Corinthians 4:14**:

> ...*He* (God) *who raised up the Lord Jesus will also raise us up with Jesus, and will present us with you.*

However, this ministry of the Holy Spirit to the believer's body also has an intermediate application in the present age. Even now, the Spirit of God, indwelling the believer, imparts to his physical body a measure of divine life and health sufficient to arrest and exclude the satanic inroads of disease and infirmity.

In **John 10:10** Christ states the supreme purpose for which He came:

> *"...I have come that they may have life, and that they may have it more abundantly."*

Someone has commented on this text, that the first portion of divine life comes through the new birth; but that the overflowing of life more abundant comes through the baptism in the Holy Spirit. It is God's purpose, even in the present age, that this divine, overflowing, abundant life from God shall suffice not merely for the spiritual needs of the inward man - that is, man's spiritual nature - but also for the physical needs of the outer man - that is, man's physical body.

In this present age the believer has not yet received his resurrection body; but he already enjoys resurrection life in a mortal body.

In **2 Corinthians 4:8-11** Paul again depicts this miracle of resurrection life in a mortal body, but he sets it against a background of tremendous pressures, both physical and spiritual:

> *We are hard pressed on every side, yet not crushed;*
> *we are perplexed, but not in despair;*
> *persecuted, but not forsaken; struck down, but not destroyed -*
> *always carrying about in the body the dying of the Lord Jesus, that the life of Jesus also may be manifested in our body.*
> *For we who live are always delivered to death for Jesus sake, that the life of Jesus also may be manifested in our mortal flesh.*

What wonderful words! The very life of Jesus is to be manifested - its presence is to be demonstrated by the visible effects which it produces *in our body.* For the sake of emphasis, Paul says this twice, but the second time he speaks of *our mortal flesh.* By this phrase, he eliminates any interpretation which might seek to apply his words to a future state of the body after resurrection. He is talking about our present physical body. In the midst of all the pressures that come against it - both natural and satanic - it is sustained by an inner life which cannot be defeated.

This manifestation of the mighty, victorious, supernatural life of the risen Christ in the believer's body is not reserved merely for the resurrection, but is to be effective even now while we still continue *in our mortal flesh.* The open manifestation of Christ's life in our body here and now is the basic, scriptural principle of divine healing and divine health.

Central to this ongoing miracle is a paradox that runs

through the whole Bible: death is the gateway to life. In each place where Paul testifies to the manifestation of Christ's life, he first speaks of identification with His death: *always carrying about in the body the dying of the Lord Jesus...*

Jesus did not die a natural death; he died by crucifixion. To be identified with Him is to be crucified with Him. But out of crucifixion comes resurrection to an inner life that owes no further debt to sin or to Satan, to the flesh or to the world.

Paul presents both the negative and the positive side of this exchange in **Galatians 2:20:**

> *"I have been crucified with Christ; it is no longer I who live, but Christ lives in me; and the life which I now live in the flesh I live by faith in the Son of God, who loved me and gave Himself for me."*

The same process of crucifixion that ends our frail, transient life in this world opens the way for a new life that is the life of God Himself, taking up residence in a vessel of clay. The vessel is still as frail as ever, but the new life in it is undefeatable and inexhaustible.

As long as this present world order continues, however, there will always be an ongoing tension between the frailty of the flesh and the new life in the Spirit. Paul sums this up in **2 Corinthians 4:16:**

> *...Even though our outward man is perishing, yet the inward man is being renewed day by day.*

The physical body is still subject to the inroads of sickness and decay from without, but the resurrection life from within has power to hold them at bay until the believer's life task is complete. After that, as Paul says in **Philippians 1:23,** *to depart and be with Christ...is far better.*

Chapter 5

DIVINE LOVE OUTPOURED

We shall devote this chapter to one final, supremely important result produced in the believer by the baptism in the Holy Spirit. It is described by Paul in the latter part of **Romans 5:5:**

> *...the love of God has been poured out in our hearts by the Holy Spirit who was given to us.*

We need to grasp the significance of that phrase: *the love of God.* Paul is not speaking here merely about human love, nor even about love for God. He is speaking about *the love of God* - that is, God's own love - which the Holy Spirit pours out in the believer's heart. This love of God, imparted by the Holy Spirit, is as high above any form of mere human love, as heaven is above earth.

As human beings, in the normal course of our lives, we encounter and experience many different forms of love. For instance, there is a form of love, so-called, which is mere sexual passion. Then there is the married love of husband and wife for each other. Again, within the human family, there is the love of parents for children, and of children for parents. Outside the bonds of the family, there is the love of one friend for another, such as the love of David and Jonathan for each other.

The Nature Of God's Love

All these, and other forms of love, in varying measure or degree, are found in all sections of the human race, even where the gospel of Christ has never been preached. The Greek language, which has an extremely rich vocabulary,

170

has various words which it uses to describe these different forms of love. There is one word, however, which is used primarily for love which is divine in its origin and nature. As a noun, this word is 'agape'; as a verb, 'agapao.'

'Agape' denotes the perfect love which exists between the Persons of the Godhead - the Father, the Son and the Spirit. It denotes the love of God toward man - that is, the love which caused God the Father to give His Son, and Christ the Son to give His life, that man might be redeemed from sin and its consequences. It denotes also the love which God, through His Holy Spirit, imparts to the hearts of those who believe in Jesus Christ.

This enables us to understand the words of the apostle in **1 John 4:7-8**:

> *Beloved, let us love one another, for love is of God; and everyone who loves is born of God and knows God. He who does not love does not know God, for God is love.*

The Greek words which John uses are 'agape' and 'agapao.' John teaches that there is a kind of love - 'agape' - which no one can experience unless he has been born of God. Love of this kind comes only from God.

Anyone who in any measure manifests this kind of love, has, in that measure, come to know God through the new birth. Conversely, a person who has never known or manifested this love in any measure, has never known God; for in the measure that any person comes to know God, he is in that measure changed and transformed by the divine love, so that he himself begins to manifest it to others.

As John here indicates, this manifestation of *agape* - of divine love - commences in human experience with the new birth. This is in harmony with the words of the apostle Peter, in **1 Peter 1:22-23**:

> *Since you have purified your souls in obeying the truth through the Spirit in sincere love of the brethren, love one another fervently with a pure heart,*
> *having been born again, not of corruptible seed but incorruptible, through the word of God which lives and abides forever...*

Where Peter says here, *love one another fervently with a pure heart,* the verb for 'love' which he uses is once again that for divine love - 'agapao.' He directly connects this possibility of Christians manifesting the divine love with the fact that they have been born again of the incorruptible seed of God's Word. That is to say, the potentiality of divine love is contained within the divine seed of God's Word implanted into their hearts at the new birth.

However, it is the purpose of God that this initial experience of divine love, received at the new birth, should thereafter be immeasurably increased and expanded through the baptism in the Holy Spirit. For this reason, Paul says, in the passage which we have already quoted, from **Romans 5:5:**

>...*the love of God has been poured out in our hearts by the Holy Spirit who was given to us.*

Once again, it is the word for divine love - 'agape' - which Paul here uses. The verb which he joins with it - *has been poured out* - is in the perfect tense. The use of the perfect tense indicates, as usual in Greek, finality and completeness. The meaning is that, in this one act of baptising the believer in the Holy Spirit, God has emptied out into the believer's heart all the fulness of the divine love. Nothing has been reserved, or held back; all has been poured out.

Through this one experience the measureless abundance of God's grace has made available to the believer all the fulness of divine love, without limitation and without reserve. Thereafter, the believer does not need to seek more of God's love; he needs only to accept, to enjoy, and to manifest, that which he has already received within.

For the Spirit-baptised believer to ask God for more of His love is like a man who lives on the immediate bank of the Mississippi or the Amazon to seek for some other supply of water. It is obvious that such a person already has at his disposal infinitely more than he can ever need to use. All that he needs is to utilise the supply already made available to him.

In like manner, Jesus says in **John 7:38-39,** the Spirit-baptised believer already has within himself not merely one river, but *rivers of living water* - rivers of divine grace and love - infinitely in excess of any need that can ever arise in that believer's life.

The precise nature of this divine love, poured out within the believer by the Holy Spirit, is defined by Paul in the next three verses of **Romans chapter 5** - that is, verses **6, 7** and **8:**

> *For when we were still without strength, in due time Christ died for the ungodly.*
>
> *For scarcely for a righteous man will one die; yet perhaps for a good man someone would even dare to die.*
>
> *But God demonstrates His own love toward us, in that while we were still sinners, Christ died for us.*

Paul points out that even natural love, apart from the grace of God, might impel a man to die for his friend, if that friend were a good and righteous man - just as natural love, in another form, might cause a mother to give her life for her child. But Paul then goes on to show that the supernatural, divine love of God is manifested in the fact that Christ died for sinners who could have had no claim upon any kind of natural love whatever.

To describe the condition of those for whom Christ died, Paul uses three successive phrases: *without strength, ungodly, sinners.* This means that those for whom Christ died were, at that time, utterly unable to help themselves, totally alienated from God, and in actual, open rebellion against God. It was in dying for people such as this that Christ manifested *agape* - the divine love - in its perfect fulness.

In **1 John 4:9,** the apostle John defines the divine love in a similar way:

> *In this the love* (agape) *of God was manifested toward us, that God has sent His only begotten Son into the world, that we might live through Him.*

The divine love does not depend upon anything worthy of love in those to whom it is directed; nor does it wait to be reciprocated before it gives all. On the contrary, it gives first, and freely, to those who are unlovable, unworthy, and even in open enmity and rebellion.

It is this divine love which is expressed in the

prayer of Jesus for those who were crucifying Him, in **Luke 23:34:**

"Father, forgive them, for they do not know what they do."

The same divine love is expressed in the dying prayer of the martyr Stephen for those who were stoning him, in **Acts 7:60:**

"Lord, do not charge them with this sin."

The same love is expressed again in the words of one who was an eager witness of Stephen's stoning - Saul of Tarsus - later, the apostle Paul. Concerning his own Jewish brethren, who had consistently rejected and persecuted him, Pauls says in **Romans 9:1-3:**

I tell the truth in Christ, I am not lying, my conscience also bearing me witness in the Holy Spirit,
that I have great sorrow and continual grief in my heart.
For I could wish that I myself were accursed from Christ for my brethren, my kinsmen according to the flesh...

So greatly did Paul yearn for the salvation of his persecuting Jewish brethren, that he would have been willing to forego all the blessings of salvation for himself and to have returned under the curse of unforgiven sin, with all its consequences, if this could have been the means of bringing his brethren to Christ. Paul acknowledges that the experience and realisation of this love was made possible only through the presence of the Holy Spirit within, for he says, *my conscience also bearing me witness **in the Holy Spirit.***

Love Is The Greatest

We have said that, amongst the various purposes for which God gives the gift of the Holy Spirit, this pouring out of divine love within the believer's heart occupies a place of unique and special importance. The reason for this is that, without the all-pervading influence of divine love in the believer's heart, all the other results which may be produced by the baptism in the Holy Spirit, lose their true significance and fail to accomplish their true purpose.

In **1 Corinthians 13:1-2** Paul uses a vivid series of examples to emphasise the unique importance of this 'agape' love:

Though I speak with the tongues of men and of angels, but have not love, I have become as sounding brass or a clanging cymbal.
And though I have the gift of prophecy, and understand all mysteries and all knowledge, and though I have all faith, so that I could remove mountains, but have not love, I am nothing.

With characteristic humility, Paul puts himself in the place of a believer who exercises spiritual gifts, but lacks divine love. In the previous chapter of **1 Corinthians,** he has enumerated nine gifts, or supernatural manifestations, of the Holy Spirit. He now imagines himself to be in the position of one exercising various of these gifts, but without love.

First, he considers the possibility of exercising the gift of tongues on such a high supernatural plane that he speaks not merely unknown human languages, but even the language of angels. He says that if he were to do this without divine love, he would be no better than a gong or a cymbal, that is capable of producing a loud noise when it is struck or rattled, but is quite empty inside.

Then he considers the possibility of exercising certain other outstanding spiritual gifts - such as prophecy, or the word of wisdom, or the word of knowledge, or faith. But he goes on to say that if he should exercise any or all of these gifts without divine love, he would be absolutely nothing.

These words of Paul here provide the answer to a question which is being asked in many circles today: is it possible to misuse the gift of tongues? The answer to this is clear: yes, it is perfectly possible to misuse the gift of tongues. Any use of tongues, apart from divine love, is a misuse, because it renders the believer who exercises it no better than an empty, clattering gong or cymbal, and this was most certainly never the purpose for which God bestowed the gift.

This applies equally to the other gifts which Paul

mentions in the next verse - that is, prophecy, the word of wisdom, the word of knowledge, and faith. To use any of these gifts apart from divine love is to miss the whole purpose of God.

However, experience proves again and again that there is a special danger of believers misusing the three spiritual gifts which operate through the organs of speech - that is, tongues, interpretation, and prophecy. This is confirmed by the fact that Paul devotes the greater part of the next chapter - that is, **1 Corinthians 14** - to giving rules to control and regulate the use of these three particular gifts. Quite obviously, if there were no possibility of believers misusing these gifts, then there would be no need to give rules for their control. The fact that rules are given proves that rules are needed.

However, in interpreting the teaching of Paul in **1 Corinthians 13:1,** it is necessary to pay close attention to the exact words which he uses. He says:

> *Though I speak with the tongues of men and of angels,*
> *but have not love, **I have become** as sounding brass*
> *or a clanging cymbal.*

Note that phrase, *I have become.* These words indicate that a change has taken place. The believer here pictured is not now in the same spiritual condition as he was when he was originally baptised in the Holy Spirit.

At that time, he had the assurance that his sins were forgiven and that his heart was cleansed through faith in Christ; and he was willing to yield himself, as fully as possible, to the control of the Holy Spirit. In this condition, the initial manifestation of speaking with another tongue indicated that the Holy Spirit had come to indwell the believer and to take control of his life.

However, in the period that has since elapsed, the believer here pictured by Paul has retained the outward manifestation, but - through carelessness, or disobedience - has not retained the same inward condition of cleansing and yieldedness to the Holy Spirit. Thus the process of speaking with tongues has degenerated into a mere outward physical manifestation, without any corresponding inward spiritual reality.

To see this experience in its proper perspective, we must set side by side two facts which are confirmed alike by Scripture and by experience.

First, at the time of being baptised in the Holy Spirit a believer must fulfil two conditions: his heart must be purified by faith in Christ; and he must be willing to yield control of his physical members - in particular, his tongue - to the Holy Spirit.

Second, the fact that the believer was, at the time of his baptism in the Spirit, cleansed and yielded is not by itself an automatic guarantee that he will always remain in that condition, even though he may still continue to exercise the manifestation of speaking in tongues.

At this point, many people are likely to exclaim: 'But surely if the person began to misuse God's gift, then God would just withdraw the gift from him altogether!'

However, this supposition that God will withdraw His gifts if they are misused, is not supported either by logic or by Scripture.

From the point of view of logic, if a gift, once given, could thereafter be withdrawn at the will of the giver, then we should have to say that it was never a genuine gift in the first instance. It was a loan, or a conditional deposit, but not a free gift. A free gift, once given, passes out of the control of the giver, and is thereafter under the sole control of the one who received it - whether to use, to abuse, or not to use at all.

This point of logic is confirmed by Scripture, for Paul says in **Romans 11:29:**

For the gifts and the calling of God are irrevocable.

This word, *irrevocable,* used here of God, and not of man, indicates that once God has given a gift, He never thereafter changes His mind and withdraws the gift again. Thereafter, the responsibility to make the proper use of the gift rests not with God, the giver, but with man, the receiver. This important principle applies in all areas of God's dealing with man, including that of the gifts of the Spirit.

This conclusion should be weighed with sober care by all those who are seeking, or who have received, the baptism in the Holy Spirit, with the manifestation of speaking with other tongues. It is not possible, according to Scripture, to receive this initial baptism without this outward manifestation. But it is possible, therafter, to have the outward manifestation without retaining the inward fulness of the Spirit.

There is only one sure, scriptural test of continuing fulness of the Holy Spirit, and that is the love test. In the measure that we are filled with the Holy Spirit, in the same measure we shall be filled with divine love. We are not more filled with the Holy Spirit than we are filled with divine love.

In **1 John 4:12-13** the apostle applies the test in clear, simple terms:

> *No one has seen God at any time. If we love one another, God abides in us, and His love has been perfected in us.*
> *By this we know that we abide in Him, and He in us...*

And again in verse **16:**

> *...God is love, and he who abides in love abides in God, and God in him.*

Likewise, in **1 Corinthians 13:13,** Paul assigns to love a place of unique honour among all God's gifts and graces:

> *And now abide faith, hope, love, these three; but the greatest of these is love.*

Of all the operations of the indwelling Spirit, the greatest and the most enduring is the pouring out of divine love in the believer's heart.

In these last four chapters we have considered the results which God desires to produce in the life of each individual believer through baptising him in the Holy Spirit. We discovered the following eight important results of this experience.

First, power to witness; second, the exalting and glorifying of Christ; third, a foretaste of heaven's power and an entrance thereby into a supernatural life; fourth, help in prayer, lifting the believer far above his own natural strength or understanding; fifth, a new understanding of the Scriptures; sixth, daily guidance in the path of God's will; seventh, life and health for the physical body; eighth, the pouring out of God's own love in the believer's heart.

In our next section we shall go on to consider results produced by this same experience in the life and worship of a Christian congregation, considered as a whole.

SECTION B: THE SPIRIT-FILLED CONGREGATION

Chapter 6

LIBERTY UNDER CONTROL

We shall now go on beyond the life of the individual believer, to consider the general life and worship of a Christian congregation as a whole. The questions which we shall seek to answer are these.

What difference does the baptism in the Holy Spirit make in the life and experience of the congregation as a whole?

What are the main features which distinguish a congregation in which all, or most, of the members have received the baptism in the Holy Spirit, and have liberty in their services to exercise the power thus received?

In what ways would such a congregation differ from one in which none of the members have received this experience?

To answer these questions, we shall examine two main ways in which a free congregation of Spirit-baptised believers differs from one in which the members have not received the baptism in the Holy Spirit.

Under The Spirit's Lordship

The first main distinguishing feature of such a congregation is indicated by Paul in **2 Corinthians 3:17**:

Now the Lord is the Spirit; and where the Spirit of the Lord is, there is liberty.

Paul here points out two important facts about the presence and influence of the Holy Spirit in a congregation. The first is that the Holy Spirit is Lord. In the New Testament the word 'Lord' corresponds in use and meaning to the name 'Jehovah' in the Old Testament. In this usage it

180

is a title reserved for the one true God, never given to any lesser being or creature.

This title belongs by right to each of the three Persons of the Godhead. God the Father is Lord; God the Son is Lord; and God the Holy Spirit is Lord. Thus, when Paul says here, *the Lord is the Spirit*, he is emphasising the supreme sovereignty of the Holy Spirit within the church.

The second great fact here pointed out by Paul is that where the Lordship of the Holy Spirit in the Church is acknowledged, the result in a congregation is 'liberty' or 'freedom.' Someone has sought to bring out the true significance of the second part of this verse by a slight change in the rendering. Instead of *where the Spirit of the Lord is, there is liberty*, we may say alternatively: 'where the Spirit is Lord, there is liberty.' That is to say, true liberty comes to a congregation in measure as its members acknowledge, and yield to, the Lordship of the Holy Spirit.

Thus, we may sum up this first main distinguishing feature of a Spirit-baptised congregation by putting two words side by side. These two words are: 'Liberty' and 'Government.'

At first sight it might appear inconsistent to put these two words together. Someone might feel inclined to object: 'But if we have liberty, then we are not under government. And if we are under government, then we do not have liberty.' People do, in fact, often feel that liberty and government are opposite to each other. This applies not merely in spiritual things, but also in the political realm.

I am reminded of the political situation in Kenya, in East Africa, while I was serving there as a College principal from 1957 to 1961. At that period the African people of Kenya were looking forward with great eagerness to the time when their country would attain to complete independence, or self-government. The Swahili word used for independence was *uhuru* - which means literally 'liberty,' or 'freedom' - and this word was upon everybody's lips. Many of the less educated Africans formed wonderful pictures of what this *uhuru*, or 'liberty,' would bring to them.

'When *uhuru* comes,' they would say, 'we shall be able to ride our bicycles on whichever side of the road we please; we shall be able to travel as far as we like in the buses without paying; we shall never have to pay any more taxes to the government.'

To more sophisticated people in other lands, statements such as these might appear childish, or ridiculous. Such people would argue that conditions such as these would not constitute true liberty, but rather anarchy and disorder in their worst degree. Nevertheless, these simple African people were perfectly sincere in the picture of 'liberty' which they had formed for themselves; and their own African political leaders often had difficulty in getting them to understand in a reasonable and practical way what liberty, or independence, really would entail.

The strange thing is that people who are perfectly sophisticated in their understanding of what political liberty means, are sometimes quite childish in the picture which they form of spiritual liberty.

Such people would smile at Africans who imagine that political liberty consists in being able to ride their bicycle on either side of the road, or in travelling in the buses without paying their fare. Yet the same people would behave in ways no less foolish or disorderly in the house of God, and then justify their behaviour by the title of 'spiritual liberty.'

For example, in some congregations, when one member is asked to lead in prayer, and to present certain definite prayer requests to God, there are others who speak so loud in other tongues that it becomes impossible for the rest of the congregation to hear what the appointed prayer leader is saying. This means that it is impossible for the congregation to say 'Amen' with understanding or faith to a prayer which they could not even hear. In this way, through this foolish misuse of tongues, the whole congregation loses the blessing and the effectiveness of united, wholehearted petition and intercession.

Or again, it may happen that the preacher is presenting a logical, scriptural message, designed to show to the unsaved the need and the way of salvation. As the preacher is approaching the climax of his message, someone in the congregation suddenly bursts out with a loud, ill-timed utterance in tongues. As a result, the attention of the whole congregation is distracted from the message of salvation; the unbelievers present are either irritated or frightened by what seems to them to be a senseless and emotional outburst; and the whole force of the carefully prepared message on salvation is lost.

If the person responsible for this kind of foolishness should afterwards be reproved, it quite often happens that he makes some such answer as this: 'I couldn't help myself! The Holy Spirit made me do it. I had to obey the Holy Spirit.' However, such an answer as this cannot be accepted, because it is contrary to the clear teaching of the Scriptures.

In **1 Corinthians 12:7,** Paul says:

> *But the manifestation of the Spirit is given to each one for the profit of all...*

We may render this more freely: 'The manifestation of the Spirit is always given for a useful, practical, sensible purpose.'

Thus, if the manifestation is directed to fulfilling the purpose for which it is given, it will always be in harmony with the plan and purpose of the service as a whole, and will make a positive contribution to accomplishing the main purpose of the service. It will never be meaningless, or distracting, or out of place.

God Makes Sons, Not Slaves

Also, in **1 Corinthians 14:32-33** Paul says:

> *And the spirits of the prophets are subject to the prophets.*
> *For God is not the author of confusion but of peace, as in all the churches of the saints.*

In other words, any spiritual manifestation that is truly directed and controlled of God, will tend to produce peace and harmony, not confusion and disorder. '

Any person responsible for a manifestation that tends towards confusion or disorder, cannot afterwards excuse himself by saying: 'I couldn't help myself! The Holy Spirit made me do it.' Paul rules out this line of defence by saying: *the spirits of the prophets are subject to the prophets.* In other words, the Holy Spirit never overrides the will of the individual believer and compels him to do something against his own will.

Even when a believer is exercising a spiritual gift, his spirit and his will still remain under his control. He is free to exercise that gift, or not to exercise it. The responsibility for exercising it remains with him. As we have said earlier in this series, the Holy Spirit never plays the part of a dictator, or a despot, in the life of a believer.

This is one of the main features which distinguish genuine manifestations of the Holy Spirit from the phenomena of spiritism, or demon possession. In many phases of spiritism, or demon possession, the person who plays the part of the medium, or other vessel of satanic power, is obliged to yield complete control of his whole will and personality to the spirit which seeks to possess him or to operate through him. Very often such a person is then obliged to say or to do things which of his own free will he would never have agreed to say or do.

In some phases of spiritism, the person who comes under the control of the spirit loses any understanding or consciousness of what he is saying or doing. At the end of such an experience as this, the possessed person may come to himself again in entirely strange surroundings after a lapse of many hours, without any knowledge or recollection of what has happened in the intervening period. In this way, both the will and the understanding of the demon possessed person are entirely set aside.

God the Holy Spirit, however, never acts in this way with the true believer in Christ. Among the most precious of all the endowments which God has bestowed upon man, His creature, are will and personality. Consequently, God never abrogates or usurps the will or the personality of the believer. He will operate through them, if He is permitted to do so, but He will never set them aside. Satan makes slaves; God makes sons.

We see, then, how wrong and unscriptural it is for Spirit-baptised believers to say concerning any spiritual manifestation: 'I couldn't help it! The Holy Spirit made me do it.' To speak like this is to represent the indwelling Spirit of God as some kind of despot, and the believer as a slave in bondage. Believers who speak like this have not yet come to understand their privileges and their responsibilities as sons of God.

They need to examine afresh the words of Paul in **Romans 8:15-16:**

> *For you did not receive the spirit of bondage* (slavery)
> *again to fear, but you received the Spirit of adoption*
> *by whom we cry out, "Abba, Father."*
> *The Spirit Himself bears witness with our spirit that*
> *we are children of God...*

We are thus brought face to face with an important general principle, which holds good in all human affairs, whether political or spiritual. True liberty is impossible without good government. The kind of liberty which seeks to set aside all government or control of any kind ends only in anarchy and confusion. The final result is a new form of slavery, far more severe than the previous form of government which was set aside.

We have seen this happen time after time in the political history of the human race; and the same principle applies equally in the spiritual life of the Christian church. True spiritual liberty is possible only where there is spiritual government. The government which God has appointed for the church is that of the Holy Spirit.

We come back therefore to the statement of Paul in **2 Corinthians 3:17:**

> *Now the Lord is the Spirit; and where the Spirit of*
> *the Lord is, there is liberty.*

If we desire to enjoy the Spirit's liberty, we must first voluntarily acknowledge the Spirit's Lordship. These two operations of the Holy Spirit can never be separated from each other.

We must also bear in mind another important fact about the Holy Spirit which we established earlier in this series. The Holy Spirit is both the author and the interpreter of the Scriptures. This means that the Holy Spirit will never direct a believer to say or do anything contrary to the

Scriptures. If the Holy Spirit were ever to do this, He would be illogical, and inconsistent with Himself; and this we know is impossible.

In **2 Corinthians 1:18-19,** Paul says:

But as God is faithful, our word to you was not Yes and No.
For the Son of God, Jesus Christ, who was preached among you by us - by me, Silvanus, and Timothy - was not Yes and No, but in Him was Yes.

Paul is here saying that God is never inconsistent with Himself. Concerning any particular matter of doctrine, or practice, God never says 'yes' at one time, and 'no' at another. If God has ever said 'yes,' then His answer always remains 'yes.' He never changes to 'no' later on. He is never changeable, or inconsistent with Himself.

This applies to the relationship between the teaching of Scripture on the one hand, and utterances and manifestations of the Holy Spirit on the other hand. The Holy Spirit, being Himself the author of Scripture, always agrees with Scripture. There is never a possibility of 'yes' and 'no.' Wherever the Bible says 'no,' the Holy Spirit says 'no.' No utterance or manifestation that is inspired and controlled by the Holy Spirit will ever be contrary to the teachings and the examples of Scripture.

However, as we have already emphasised, the Holy Spirit in the life of the believer is not a dictator. He does not compel the believer always to act in a scriptural way. The Holy Spirit serves as interpreter and counsellor. He interprets the Scripture; He offers direction and counsel. But the believer still remains free to accept or to reject the Holy Spirit's counsel - to obey, or to disobey.

This imposes a tremendous responsibility upon every Spirit-baptised believer. Every such believer is responsible to acquaint himself personally with the mind of the Holy Spirit as revealed in the Scriptures, and then to direct his own conduct and behaviour in regard to the exercise of spiritual gifts or manifestations - as in all other matters - so that these harmonise with the principles and examples of Scripture.

If through laziness, indifference, or disobedience, a Spirit-baptised believer fails to do this, and as a result exercises spiritual gifts or manifestations in a foolish and unscriptural way, the responsibility for this rests solely upon the believer himself, not upon the Holy Spirit.

In this connection, a special responsibility rests upon every minister called by God to lead the worship and service of a Spirit-baptised congregation. Not only must such a man direct his own spiritual ministry in line with the teaching of Scripture; he must also allow himself to be, in God's hand, an instrument to direct the worship and ministry of the whole congregation in accordance with the same scriptural principles.

To do this successfully requires, in a high degree, certain special qualifications: first of all, a thorough practical knowledge of the Scriptures; and then wisdom, authority, and courage. Where these qualities are lacking in the leadership, a congregation that seeks to exercise spiritual gifts and manifestations will be like a ship at sea, in the midst of powerful winds and treacherous shoals, with an ill-trained and inexperienced captain in charge. Small wonder if the end is a wreck!

I have now been personally associated with full gospel ministry continuously for more than forty years. During those years I have observed two things which have done more than anything else to hinder the acceptance of the testimony of the full gospel. The first is the failure to exercise proper control over the public manifestation of spiritual gifts, particularly the gift of tongues; the second is strife and division amongst Spirit-baptised believers, both amongst members of the same congregation, and between one congregation and another. Each of these things has its origin in one and the same error: the failure to acknowledge the effective Lordship of the Holy Spirit.

We are now in a position to offer a definition of true spiritual liberty. Spiritual liberty consists in just this one thing: acknowledging the effective Lordship of the Holy Spirit in the Church. Where the Spirit is Lord, there is liberty.

Times And Seasons

So many Spirit-baptised believers have their own particular concept of liberty. Some imagine that liberty consists in shouting. If only we can shout loud enough and long enough, they seem to think, we shall work ourselves up into liberty. But the Holy Spirit is never worked up; He either comes down, or He flows forth from within. In either case, His manifestation is free and spontaneous, never laborious or wearisome.

Other Spirit-baptised believers lay all their emphasis on some other type of expression, or manifestation; such as singing, or clapping hands, or dancing. In many cases the reason for this is that God once blessed them along one of these lines, and they have come to believe that God's blessing will always continue to come along this same line, and never along any other. God blessed them once shouting, so they always want to shout. Or God blessed them once dancing, so they always want to dance.

They have become so limited in their outlook and in their concept of the Holy Spirit, that they can never conceive of God blessing them in any other way. Quite often, they even tend to despise other believers who will not join them in their shouting, or their dancing, or their clapping hands, and to suggest that these other believers are not really 'free in the Spirit.'

Let us be careful to add that there is not necessarily anything unscriptural in shouting, or dancing, or clapping hands. The Bible provides clear examples of all these things in the worship of God's people. But it certainly is unscriptural, and also foolish, to suggest that any of these forms of expression necessarily constitute true spiritual liberty.

A person who imagines that he must always worship God by shouting, or dancing, or clapping hands, no longer enjoys true spiritual liberty; on the contrary, he has returned under a special kind of religious bondage, of his own making. Such a person is as much under bondage as the Christian at the opposite end of the religious scale, who knows of no other way to worship God than with the words and forms of a printed liturgy.

A wonderful key to true spiritual liberty is found in the words of Solomon in **Ecclesiastes 3:1-8:**

To everything there is a season,
A time for every purpose under heaven:
A time to be born,
And a time to die;
A time to plant,
And a time to pluck what is planted;
A time to kill,
And a time to heal;
A time to break down,
And a time to build up;
A time to weep,
And a time to laugh;
A time to mourn,
And a time to dance;
A time to cast away stones,
And a time to gather stones;
A time to embrace,
And a time to refrain from embracing;
A time to gain,
And a time to lose;
A time to keep,
And a time to throw away;
A time to tear,
And a time to sew;
A time to keep silence,
And a time to speak;
A time to love,
And a time to hate;
A time of war,
And a time of peace.

Solomon here mentions twenty-eight forms of activity, set out in fourteen pairs of opposites. In each pair of opposites, it is right at one time to do the one, and at another time to do the other. We can never say absolutely, without qualification, it is always right to do the one, or always wrong to do the other. Whether each is right or wrong, is decided by the time, or the season.

In these pairs of opposites which Solomon mentions, there are many which relate to the life and worship of a congregation; such as planting, or plucking up; killing, or healing; breaking down, or building up; weeping, or laughing; mourning, or dancing; gathering, or casting away; keeping silence, or speaking.

None of these is either absolutely right, or absolutely wrong. Each is right if done at the right time, and wrong if done at the wrong time.

How then shall we know which to do, or when? The answer is: this is the sovereign office of the Holy Spirit, as Lord in the church. He reveals and directs what to do, and when. A congregation that is directed by the Holy Spirit will do the right thing at the right time. This is the source of all true liberty, harmony, and unity. Apart from this, there are only varying degrees of bondage, discord, and disunity.

In the next chapter we shall go on to consider one further important distinctive feature that marks the life and worship of a congregation where the members have been baptised in the Holy Spirit and have liberty to exercise this power.

Chapter 7

TOTAL PARTICIPATION OF THE MEMBERS

We shall now go on to examine a second distinctive and important feature of a Spirit-filled congregation.

In the regular services of the great majority of Christian churches today, almost all the real initiative and activity are confined to just a few individuals. The congregation as a whole may take part in certain pre-arranged activities, such as the singing of hymns from a book, the repetition of fixed prayers, or responses. There may also be, within the main congregation, one or two smaller, specially trained groups - such as the choir, or an orchestra. But apart from this, in the majority of congregations, all real initiative and activity are left in the hands of one or two individuals, while the rest of the congregation remain mainly passive.

One person leads the singing; one person prays; one person preaches. Sometimes two or more, even of these activities, may be combined in one person. From the rest of the congregation little more is expected or required than an occasional 'Amen.'

However, if we examine with an open mind the life and worship of the early church, as portrayed in the New Testament, we find that there was active participation by all the believers present in any service; and that this was brought about by the supernatural presence and power of the Holy Spirit, operating in and through the individual believers.

The Lamp On The Lampstand

Further study of this New Testament pattern reveals that the supernatural gifts or manifestations of the Holy Spirit are not given primarily to the individual believer. Rather,

191

they are given, through the vessel of the individual believer, to the church or congregation as a whole. Therefore they cannot achieve their proper purpose, unless they are freely manifested and exercised in the life of the congregation.

In **1 Corinthians 12** Paul indicates how the gifts of the individual believers are intended to function within the corporate life of the whole congregation.

First of all, in verses **7-11,** he lists nine specific supernatural gifts, or manifestations, of the Holy Spirit, ending with the words:

> *But one and the same Spirit works all these things, distributing to each one individually as He wills.*

This last phrase obviously indicates that these gifts, or manifestations, are given in the first instance to individual believers. However, Paul does not end there.

In the next 16 verses of the same chapter - that is, verses **12-27** - Paul goes on to say that the Christian church is like one body with many members, and he likens each individual believer to a single member of the one body, ending with the words: *Now you are the body of Christ, and members individually.*

The lesson therefore is that, though the spiritual gifts are given to individual believers, they are given for the purpose of enabling those believers to play their proper part in the Church - the body of Christ - as a whole. Thus spiritual gifts are not intended primarily for the benefit of the individual, but for the life and worship of the whole congregation.

Paul makes the same point again in the very next verse - that is, **1 Corinthians 12:28:**

> *And God has appointed these in the church: first apostles, second prophets, third teachers, after that miracles, then gifts of healings, helps, administrations, varieties of tongues.*

Speaking here of various ministries and supernatural gifts of the Holy Spirit, Paul says, concerning all of them, that they have been set by God *in the church*. That is, they are intended not merely for private use by individual believers, but for public manifestation in the church - the congregation of God's people as a whole.

This same truth is vividly illustrated by a brief parable which Jesus relates in **Matthew 5:15:**

"Nor do they light a lamp and put it under a basket, but on a lampstand, and it gives light to all who are in the house."

The two main symbols used in this parable are the lamp and the lampstand. The symbol of the lampstand may be interpreted by reference to **Revelation 1:20:**

"...the seven lampstands which you saw are the seven churches."

Throughout the whole of Scripture, a lampstand is used as a symbol of a church or a congregation.

The symbol of the lighted lamp may be interpreted by reference to **Proverbs 20:27:**

The spirit of a man is the lamp of the Lord...

Thus the lighted lamp is a symbol of the spirit of the Spirit-baptised believer, made to burn and to shine by the fire of the indwelling Spirit.

Just as the lamp is appointed to take its place on the lampstand, so the Spirit-baptised believer is appointed to take his place in the public congregation of the Church. A believer who has been baptised in the Holy Spirit, but never exercises any spiritual gift in the service of the congreation, is like a lamp under a basket. He fails to fulfil the purpose for which God gave him the gift.

We see then, from these Scriptures, that the supernatural gifts of the Holy Spirit are not intended merely for the private use or enjoyment of the individual believer. On the contrary, they are intended to play an effective part in the public life and worship of the congregation as a whole.

When the presence and power of the Holy Spirit are publicly manifested in this way through the various believers, the whole life and worship of the congregation are completely transformed. The main responsibility for the ministry and the conduct of the service is no longer borne by one or two individuals, while the rest remain passive. On the contrary, every member of the congregation begins to participate actively in the service, and the various members minister to each other, rather than one or two ministering all the time to all the rest.

This is the pattern indicated by Paul's example of the body and its members, and it is confirmed by the words of the apostle Peter, in **1 Peter 4:10-11:**

> *As each one has received a gift, minister it to one another, as good stewards of the manifold grace of God. If anyone speaks, let him speak as the oracles of God. If anyone ministers, let him do it as with the ability which God supplies, that in all things God may be glorified through Jesus Christ...*

Peter here speaks of God's grace being *manifold*. That is, God's grace is so rich - so many-sided - that a different aspect of that grace can be manifested through each individual member in the total worship and service of God's people. In this way every member of the church may receive his own special manifestation, and may thus have something to minister in turn to all the other members.

Peter emphasises that every member of the church is included; no one need be left without a gift, or a ministry. He says: *As each one has received a gift, minister it to one another...* And again, in the next verse: *If anyone speaks...If anyone ministers...* There is no question here of a church with one or two 'professional,' full time ministers, while all the remaining members are largely passive, or inactive. Every member is included in God's programme of supernatural ministry in the church; each one may have a gift; anyone may speak; anyone may minister.

This picture of the church with every member active is confirmed by the words of Paul, in **Romans 12:3-8:**

> *For I say, through the grace given to me, to everyone who is among you, not to think of himself more highly than he ought to think, but to think soberly, as God has dealt to each one a measure of faith.*
> *For as we have many members in one body, but all the members do not have the same function,*
> *so we, being many, are one body in Christ, and individually members of one another.*

*Having then gifts differing according to the grace that
is given to us, let us prophecy in proportion to our faith;
or ministry, let us use it in our ministering; he who
teaches, in teaching;
he who exhorts, in exhortation; he who gives, with
liberality; he who leads, with diligence; he who shows
mercy, with cheerfulness.*

In these verses Paul once again likens the Christian
Church to a body, of which each individual believer is a
member, and he lays great stress on the activity of each
member. Notice the repetition of phrases such as; *each one,
all the members, everyone.*

Paul teaches that God has allotted to each member a
special function, a special ministry. In conjunction with this,
God has also made a double provision for the effective exercise of that ministry: first, the measure of faith and,
second, the special gifts which the ministry requires. In this
way each member is fully equipped for his task.

Thus, the New Testament picture of the church is that
of a vigorous, active body, in which each believer, each individual member, properly fulfills his special function. A
church in which only one or two members had any active
ministry would be, by New Testament standards, like a body
in which, let us say, the head, one hand, and one foot were
strong and active, and all the rest of the body was paralysed
and useless. Obviously such a body, considered as a whole,
could never fulfill its proper function.

In **1 Corinthians 12:7** and **11,** Paul lays particular
emphasis upon the supernatural ministry imparted by the
Holy Spirit to every member of a New Testament church:

*But the manifestation of the Spirit is given to each one
for the profit of all...*

And again, concerning the nine supernatural gifts of the
Holy Spirit:

*But one and the same Spirit works all these things,
distributing to each one individually as He wills.*

Notice carefully what Paul says here: '...the manifestation
of the Spirit (that is, the manifest, public demonstration of

the indwelling Spirit) *is given to each one* (that is, to every member of the church). And again: all these nine supernatural gifts, the Holy Spirit distributes *to each one individually* (that is, to every member).

The Exercise Of Spiritual Gifts

These words make it plain that it is the express will of God for every member of the church to exercise spiritual gifts - that is, the open, public, supernatural manifestation of the indwelling Spirit. If all believers do not in fact have these gifts in operation, it is not because God withholds them, but simply because such believers through ignorance, or carelessness, or unbelief, fail to press on into the fulness of God's revealed will for His people.

Such believers have failed to obey the exhortation of Paul in **1 Corinthians 12:31:**

But earnestly desire the best gifts...

And again in **1 Corinthians 14:1:**

Pursue love, and desire spiritual gifts, but especially that you may prophesy.

There are three spiritual gifts about which Paul is particularly specific: tongues, interpretation, and prophecy.

In **1 Corinthians 14:5,** he says:

I wish you all spoke with tongues, but even more that you prophesied...

Since Paul is here writing under the inspiration of the Holy Spirit, his words impart to the Church the revealed will of God for all His believing people both to speak with tongues, and to prophesy. If there are believers who do not enjoy the exercise of these gifts, it is not because God has withheld them, but simply because those believers have not entered into the fulness of their inheritance in Christ.

In **Joshua 13:1,** the Lord said to Joshua and to His people under the old covenant:

"...there remains very much land yet to be possessed."

So it is also with God's people under the new covenant today:

"...there remains very much land yet to be possessed."

In **1 Corinthians 14:13,** Paul says also:

Therefore let him who speaks in a tongue pray that he may interpret.

Obviously, God's Word does not tell us to pray for something which it is not God's will for us to have. Therefore, we know that it is God's will for anyone who speaks in tongues also to interpret that utterance. Since Paul has already said that it is God's will for all to speak in tongues, it is therefore also God's will for all to interpret.

Again, in **1 Corinthians 14:31,** Paul says:

For you can all prophesy one by one, that all may learn and all may be encouraged.

Nothing could be plainer than this. It is within the revealed will of God for all the members of the church to exercise the spiritual gift of prophesy. On this general revelation of God's will, Paul imposes only two limitations. Here in the verse just quoted, he says, *one by one*. That is, believers are to exercise this gift by turns, not more than one believer prophesying at any one time. The purpose of this is obvious, and is stated a few verses further on. It is, to avoid confusion.

The other limitation upon the exercise of the gift of prophecy is stated by Paul a little earlier, in **1 Corinthians 14:29:**

Let two or three prophets speak, and let the others (that is, the other members) *judge.*

Paul here limits the number who may exercise the gift of prophecy in any service. He says, *two or three*. The purpose of this is that the whole service should not be monopolised by one particular form of spiritual manifestation. The exercise of prophecy has its place in the service, but it does not make up the whole service. The ministry of the Holy Spirit through God's people is much more varied than that. Many other different forms of ministry are required to make up a complete service.

In this verse Paul also says clearly that the exercise of the gift of prophecy must be judged, or tested. He says: *let the others judge*. The *others* would include the rest of the Spirit-baptised believers present, who are capable of recognising the genuine manifestation of the gift of prophecy. Even in this we see that Paul brings in all the members. He does not specify merely one professional minister who is to judge, but he makes the believers as a whole responsible to do this.

This is in line with what Paul says in **1 Thessalonians 5:19-21:**

> *Do not quench the Spirit.*
> *Do not despise prophecies.*
> *Test all things; hold fast what is good.*

These three verses are addressed to Christian believers generally, and they must be taken closely together. It is wrong for believers to quench the Spirit - that is, to reject the moving and manifestation of the Holy Spirit in their midst. It is also wrong for believers to despise prophesyings - that is, to adopt an attitude of criticism, contempt, or unbelief towards the manifestation of the gift of prophecy.

On the other hand, when this gift is manifested, believers are responsible to test it by the standards of Scripture - and then to hold fast, to accept, to retain, only that which is good - only that which accords with the standards and patterns of Scripture.

We see, then, that Paul is careful to guard against anything that might be spurious, or disorderly, in the exercise or manifestation of spiritual gifts. However, with this one qualification, he repeatedly and emphatically states that all believers in the church can, and should, enjoy and exercise the open manifestation of spiritual gifts. In this connection, he particularly specifies the three gifts of tongues, interpretation, and prophecy.

What is the result in a church when all its members freely and publicly exercise supernatural spiritual gifts in this way?

In **1 Corinthians 14:26,** Paul describes the kind of services which result from this:

> *How is it then, brethren? Whenever you come together, each of you has a psalm, has a teaching, has a tongue, has a revelation, has an interpretation. Let all things be done for edification.*

That phrase *each of you has* sets a pattern. It implies active participation by all the members.

Generally speaking, when Christians come together today, they do so with the primary purpose of receiving, not of contributing. They come to get a blessing, to receive healing, to hear a preacher.

But this was not the way of the New Testament church. There the members came not primarily to receive, but to contribute. Every one of them had something committed to him individually by the Holy Spirit which he was in turn able to contribute to the total worship and service of the church.

Paul mentions various possible forms of contribution. *A psalm* would denote some form of musical contribution. This might be the product either of natural talent, or of the supernatural enabling of the Holy Spirit. *A teaching* would denote the ability to impart some truth from the teaching of God's Word. *A tongue* and *an interpretation* might be taken to cover generally the three gifts of supernatural utterance - tongues, interpretation, and prophecy. *A revelation* would cover any one of the three main revelatory gifts - 'the word of wisdom,' 'the word of knowledge' and 'discernment of spirits.'

In this way - mainly through the operation of the supernatural spiritual gifts - all the members had something of their own to contribute towards the total worship and service of the church. They were thus able to fulfill the injunction given by Peter in **1 Peter 4:10**:

> As each one has received a gift, minister it to one another...

Peter brings out the same point as Paul. The ability of the members to minister effectively to one another was due mainly to the fact that they had received these supernatural spiritual gifts. They were thus lifted out of the limitations of their own education or natural talent, into a much higher realm of spiritual freedom.

Had their ability to minister to each other depended merely on education or natural talent, many of them would have been left with very little to contribute. The result would have been just what we see in the majority of churches today. The main burden of ministry would have fallen upon just a few of the members, while the rest would have remained largely passive, or inactive, without any real opportunities for spiritual expression or development.

Why is it that so many professional ministers in our modern churches suffer mental or nervous breakdowns?

The answer is that, in many cases, one member is struggling to carry a burden of ministry which God never laid upon him. One member is seeking to fulfil a ministry which God intended should be divided up amongst all the members in the church. The almost inevitable result is some kind of breakdown.

The only escape from the limitations and frustrations of this situation is through the supernatural ministry of the Holy Spirit in the church, dividing spiritual gifts to all the members individually, according to His own will. This delivers believers from their own natural limitations and lifts them into a spiritual realm where they can share together the burden of the total ministry of the church.

When all the members are thus equipped to function in their individual ministries, the church as a whole can fulfil its corporate role as the body of Christ.

SECTION C: THE SPIRIT-FILLED PREACHER

Chapter 8

CONVICTION OF ETERNAL ISSUES

In the last two chapters we considered the effects produced by the baptism in the Holy Spirit upon the general life and worship of a Christian congregation as a whole.

We shall now focus our attention upon the special ministry of the preacher - that is, the believer called by God to the vital ministry of preaching God's Word. The questions which we shall seek to answer are these.

What special results are produced in the ministry of the preacher by the baptism in the Holy Spirit?

In what main ways does the ministry of a preacher who is empowered by the Holy Spirit differ from that of one who is not?

In considering the relationship between the Holy Spirit and the ministry of the preacher, it is appropriate to begin with the words of the apostle in **1 Peter 1:12.** Peter here reminds the early church of the example and the standard set before them by the preachers who had brought the gospel message to them. He speaks of those *who have preached the gospel to you by the Holy Spirit sent from heaven...*

These words bring out clearly the main distinctive feature of the New Testament preachers. They did not depend primarily upon education, or eloquence, or natural talents; they preached *by the Holy Spirit sent from heaven.* They reckoned and depended upon the real, personal presence and power of the Holy Spirit working in them, through them, and with them. Every other means and talent that they employed was kept subservient to this one controlling influence - the presence and power of the Holy Spirit.

What are the results which follow when the preeminence of the Holy Spirit is thus acknowledged in the ministry of the preacher?

Sin, Righteousness And Judgment

The first such result is stated by Jesus in **John 16:8**:

"And when He (the Holy Spirit) *has come, He will convict the world of sin, and of righteousness, and of judgment..."*

An alternative translation for *convict* is 'convince.' *He will convince the world of sin, and of righteousness, and of judgment...*

We might paraphrase this: 'The Holy Spirit will press home upon the attention of the unbelieving world the true basic issues of sin, righteousness, and judgment, in such a way that it will no longer be possible for the world to ignore, or deny, these issues.'

These three things - sin, righteousness, and judgment - are the abiding eternal realities upon which all true religion is based.

In **Acts 17:31,** Paul reminds the proud, intellectual, self-sufficient Athenian people of this basic issue of God's judgment:

"...(God) *has appointed a day on which He will judge the world in righteousness..."*

Judgment is a divine appointment; none are excused; none are exempted; none can escape. God's appointment is with the world - the entire human race. In this judgment, God is concerned with one issue, and only one: that is the issue of righteousness. God will not judge men in respect of their wealth, or of their cleverness, or of their religious profession. He is concerned about one issue only: that of righteousness.

The nature of this issue is clearly defined by the apostle in **1 John 5:17:** *All unrighteousness is sin...* In respect of moral conduct, there is only one alternative to righteousness - and that is sin. Sin must be defined in terms of righteousness. The negative must be defined in terms of the positive.

It is as if we should be asked to explain the word

'crooked.' The simplest way to do this would be to begin by demonstrating the meaning of 'straight.' We could draw a straight line, and say: 'This is straight.' Then we could go on to say: 'Any other line extending between the same two points, that does not follow the course of this line, is crooked.'

The exact extent to which the crooked line deviates from the straight is a matter of quite secondary importance. It may deviate by one degree, or it may deviate many degrees. This makes no difference. Whether it deviates by little or by much, it is still crooked.

So it is with the issue of sin and of righteousness. All unrighteousness is sin. Every form of moral conduct that is not righteous is sinful. God has established His divine standard of righteousness. Anything which departs from that in any degree, small or great, is sinful.

What is God's standard of righteousness? The answer to this is given in the second part of the verse which we have already quoted from Paul's speech at Athens - that is, in **Acts 17:31:**

> "...because He has appointed a day on which He will judge the world in righteousness by the Man whom He has ordained. He has given assurance of this to all by raising Him from the dead."

What is God's standard of righteousness, here stated? It is not a moral code, nor a golden rule; not even the ten commandments. It is the one kind of standard perfectly suited to the human race. It is **a man** - that man whom God has ordained.

Who is this man? It is the man to whom God has given testimony, or assurance, by raising him from the dead. It is the man Jesus Christ. He and He alone is God's standard of righteousness for the human race. To understand this standard we must study the life and the character of Jesus, as portrayed in the New Testament. Every aspect of human character or conduct that falls below the standard of Jesus falls below God's standard of righteousness.

In a different form of words, Paul presents the same

truth concerning the nature of righteousness and sin in **Romans 3:23:**

> *...for all have sinned and fall short of the glory of God...*

Here in asserting the universal sinfulness of the entire human race, Paul does not specify any one particular type of sin. He does not specify pride, or lust, or murder, or lies. There is only one point in which he asserts that all are alike guilty: all have come short of the glory of God. All have failed to live for God's glory; all have failed to live up to the divine standard; all have come short; all have missed the mark.

This standard of God's glory points us once again to Jesus Christ. For in **Hebrews 1:3,** we are told that He, Jesus, is both

> *...the brightness of His* (the Father's) *glory and the express image of His person...*

Jesus Christ alone, of all men who have ever lived, lived out His entire life by this one standard and for this one purpose - the glory of God, His Father.

Here then, defined and demonstrated for all to see, are the three basic issues upon which the eternal destiny of every human soul depends - the issues of sin, righteousness, and judgment.

Yet the human race, in its own natural, unregenerate condition, is totally unconcerned about these issues. This is because fallen man is the slave of his own carnal mind. He has only one normal means of contact with reality, and that is through his fleshly nature - through his five senses. He is moved and impressed only by the aspects of reality which are revealed to him by his senses. He is therefore shut up in the realm of the carnal and of the material. It is the things in this realm which impress him and influence him, which occupy his time, his thoughts, his energy.

Listen to people of the world talking casually together in any public place - a bus, a train, a restaurant. What is the commonest topic of conversation? Without a doubt, it is money. I have proved this by personal observation, listening to people talk in many different languages and in many different lands.

After money there come a variety of other topics, all connected in some way with man's physical and material well-being, his pleasures, his comforts, his luxuries. Amongst the commonest of these topics right round the world we might mention: sport; entertainment; politics; food; business; farming; family affairs; cars; clothing and household equipment.

These are the things which normally monopolise the thought and the speech of the people of this world. Amongst them no place is found for the three issues which we have mentioned - sin, righteousness, and judgment.

Why is this? The answer is simple. These three things cannot be apprehended through man's carnal senses. For the man who is shut up within the prison of his own senses and his own carnal understanding, sin, righteousness, and judgment have no reality or importance whatever.

There is only one means by which these things can be made real for men and women, and that is through the working of God's Holy Spirit. He alone can convince the world of these unseen, eternal realities. In proportion as the Holy Spirit gains access to men's hearts and minds, they become convinced and concerned about sin, about righteousness, and about judgment.

In **Psalm 14:2-3,** we are given a divinely inspired picture of the whole human race, as God Himself sees them, in their own natural, fallen condition, apart from the influence of God's grace and the working of God's Spirit. The Psalmist here says:

> *The Lord looks down from heaven upon the children of men,*
> *To see if there are any who understand, who seek God.*
> *They have all turned aside,*
> *They have together become corrupt;*
> *There is none who does good,*
> *No, not one.*

Notice what the Psalmist here says about man's natural condition. It is not merely that there is none who does good. Man's spiritual depravity goes much deeper than that. There is none who understands, none who seeks God. Even the

205

understanding of spiritual things and the desire to know God are totally absent. Until God through His Holy Spirit reaches down to man, man, left to himself, never reaches out to God, or seeks after God.

This agrees with what Paul says in **Ephesians 2:1:**

And you He made alive, who were dead in trespasses and sins...

Apart from the quickening influence of the Holy Spirit, man's spiritual condition is one of death. He is dead to God, and to spiritual realities. Sin, righteousness, and judgment have no meaning or reality for him.

This does not mean that man in this condition is necessarily without religion. On the contrary, religion may play a great part in his life. But religion, apart from the moving of the Holy Spirit, can be the most deadening of all influences, lulling man into a false sense of security and into callousness and indifference concerning those vital spiritual issues upon which the destiny of his soul depends.

In **2 Timothy 3:1-5,** Paul gives a prophetic picture of the main moral features which will characterise the human race at the close of the present age:

But know this, that in the last days perilous times will come:
For men will be lovers of themselves, lovers of money, boasters, proud, blasphemers, disobedient to parents, unthankful, unholy,
unloving, unforgiving, slanderers, without self-control, brutal, despisers of good,
traitors, headstrong, haughty, lovers of pleasure rather than lovers of God,
having a form of godliness but denying its power. And from such people turn away!

Paul here lists eighteen major moral blemishes that will mar and disfigure human life and conduct as this age draws to its close. The first two such moral blemishes in his list are *lovers of themselves* and *lovers of money;* the last in the list is *lovers of pleasures rather than lovers of God.* By the unerring insight of the Holy Spirit Paul has pointed out three major marks of our contemporary civilisation: 'love of self,' 'love of money,' 'love of pleasure.'

In between these are fifteen other features of moral decline, all of which have been manifested in the twentieth century more openly and on a larger scale than at any previous period of world history.

Yet the most challenging aspect of this whole situation is that, in the midst of this universal moral decline, there is no absence of religion. After listing these eighteen moral blemishes, Paul adds, *having a form of godliness, but denying its power.*

In other words, the people guilty of these moral sins are not people without religion. They have a *form of godliness* - a form of religion - but it is a religion in which there is no room for the presence and power of the Holy Spirit. As a result, there is no sensitiveness to spiritual things; no awareness of basic spiritual realities; no conviction of sin, or of righteousness, or of judgment.

It follows from this that to preach the gospel message of salvation through Christ, without the accompanying influence of the Holy Spirit, is a totally useless endeavour. It is presenting a remedy to people who have no consciousness of a need - a cure to people who have no consciousness of being sick. The only reaction which this can produce is one of indifference, or scorn.

The greatest enemy of evangelistic activity is not communism, nor false cults. It is materialism, and indifference. The only power that can break down this barrier of materialism is the power of the Holy Spirit. *"When He* (the Holy Spirit) *has come, He will convict the world of sin, and of righteousness, and of judgment."*

It is not mere preaching that the world needs - it is preaching like that of the early church - preaching *by the Holy Spirit sent from heaven.*

Wielding The Spirit's Sword

Let us look briefly at the examples of this type of preaching recorded in the book of Acts, and at the results which it produced.

On the day of Pentecost, before the coming of the Holy Spirit, the 120 believers in the upper room in Jerusalem were an unimpressive, uninfluential minority. But after they had been filled with the Holy Spirit, Peter stood up and preached a sermon to a crowd of several thousand Jewish people who had gathered. What were the results of this one sermon? They are recorded in **Acts 2:37:**

> *Now when they heard this, they were cut to the heart, and said to Peter and the rest of the apostles, "Men and brethren, what shall we do?"*

Notice that significant phrase: *they were cut to the heart...* This cutting to the heart is the operation of the Holy Spirit which Jesus prophetically foreshowed, when he said;

> *...when He* (the Holy Spirit) *has come, He will convict the world of sin, and of righteousness, and of judgment...*

As a result of this conviction, before the day closed, three thousand of these unbelieving Jews had repented, had acknowledged Jesus as Lord and Saviour, and had obediently followed him through the waters of baptism.

However, it is important to emphasise that these results were not achieved merely by the supernatural manifestation of the Holy Spirit alone, but by this manifestation followed by the preaching of God's Word. In **1 Corinthians 1:21,** Paul says:

> *...it pleased God through the foolishness of the message preached to save those who believe.*

God has never ordained that men should be saved through witnessing miracles or through hearing prophetic utterances. These supernatural manifestations serve to arrest men's attention and to open their hearts to the truth. But it is only through the preaching of God's Word that men are actually saved.

This serves to illustrate the statement of Paul in **Ephesians 6:17,** that *the sword of the Spirit is the Word of God...*

If Peter had not stood up on the day of Pentecost and preached a message from God's Word, the Holy Spirit would still have been mightily present and with the disciples. But He would have been left without any sword to wield. There would still have been awe and amazement on the part of the unbelievers, but there would have been no conversions. It was the sharp, two-edged sword of God's Word, wielded by the Holy Spirit through the lips of Peter, that cut these unbelievers right to their hearts and brought them under such deep conviction.

In studying Peter's sermon on the day of Pentecost, it is illuminating to discover that almost half of it consists of actual quotations from the Old Testament Scriptures. So great is the impact of God's written word, when it is pressed home to the human heart by the power of the Holy Spirit.

In Acts chapters 6 and 7 we read how Stephen was accused of blasphemy and arraigned before the Jewish council in Jerusalem. At the opening of the trial scene, Stephen is accused, and the members of the council are the accusers. But before the trial closes, these roles have been reversed.

As Stephen, under the anointing of the Holy Spirit, expounds to the council the Old Testament Scriptures relating to Israel and to the Messiah, it is Stephen who becomes the accuser, and the members of the council who are accused. The effect of Stephen's words upon the council is described in **Acts 7:54:**

When they heard these things they were cut to the heart, and they gnashed at him with their teeth.

Notice the same phrase again: *cut to the heart.*

Once more, we see that the sword of God's Word, wielded by the Holy Spirit, reached right home to the hearts of those unbelievers, and wounded them there most deeply.

One of the witnesses of Stephen's trial and martyrdom was a young man named Saul of Tarsus. In **Acts 9:5,** we read of the effect produced by these events upon Saul. For when Jesus appeared to him later on the Damascus road, He said:

"...It is hard for you to kick against the goads."

What were these goads from which Saul was seeking vainly to escape? They were the sharp goads of God's Word, that had been pressed home to his heart by the Holy Spirit through the lips of Stephen.

Acts 24 describes another trial, in which Paul was now

the accused, arraigned concerning his faith in Christ, and the Roman governor, Felix, was the judge. In this trial, once again, the Holy Spirit reversed the roles of accuser and accused. For we read in **Acts 24:25,** that as Paul *reasoned about righteousness, self-control, and the judgment to come, Felix was afraid...* As the Holy Spirit, through Paul, pressed home to the heart of Felix these truths of righteousness and judgment, the proud Roman governor, accustomed to have prisoners tremble before him, found himself trembling in the presence of an unseen judge, and hastily dismissed the court, without any judgment being pronounced.

These examples from the book of Acts illustrate the supernatural power of the Holy Spirit to convict men of sin, of righteousness, and of judgment. But they also show that conviction is not the same as conversion, nor does it necessarily lead to conversion. There is one thing, however, that the Holy Spirit, by His convicting power, most surely does: He leaves no further room for neutrality.

In **Matthew 12:30,** Jesus says:

> *"He who is not with Me is against Me, and he who does not gather with Me scatters abroad."*

Where the convicting power of the Holy Spirit is manifested, every person that comes under the influence of that power is compelled to take a definite stand - either with Christ, or against Him, either gathering, or scattering. Compromise, or neutrality, are no longer possible.

It was with reference to this also that Jesus said, in **Matthew 10:34-35:**

> *"Do not think that I came to bring peace on earth. I did not come to bring peace but a sword.*
> *For I have come to 'set a man against his father, a daughter against her mother, and a daughter-in-law against her mother-in-law.'"*

The *sword* of which Jesus here speaks is the sword of God's Word. As this Word is ministered in the power of the Holy Spirit, it is so sharp and so penetrating that it leaves no place any more for neutrality, or compromise. It divides even amongst members of the same family, compelling each one individually to take a stand, either with Christ or against Him.

We live in a civilisation that is marked by materialism, indifference, compromise, moral and spiritual decline. Is there anything that can arrest the course of this decline, and turn our generation back to God?

Yes, there is one thing that can do this, and only one: the power of the Holy Spirit, working through the Word of God, convincing the world of sin, of righteousness, and of judgment.

Chapter 9

SUPERNATURAL ATTESTATION

We shall now examine one further important result produced by the baptism in the Holy Spirit in the ministry of
the preacher. This is described in **Hebrews 2:3-4:**

> *...how shall we escape if we neglect so great a salva-
> tion, which at the first began to be spoken by the Lord,
> and was confirmed to us by those who heard Him,
> God also bearing witness both with signs and wonders,
> with various miracles, and gifts of the Holy Spirit,
> according to His own will?*

The writer here states three reasons why the gospel
message should command the most careful attention of all
who hear it. First, because it was preached initially by the
Lord Jesus Christ Himself; second, because the message was
then transmitted and recorded by men who themselves
heard and saw all that took place; third, because this
message, so transmitted, was further supernaturally attested
by the signs and wonders, miracles and gifts of the Holy
Spirit which accompanied the message.

From this we see that one main ministry of the Holy
Spirit, in relation to the preaching of the gospel, is to bear
supernatural testimony, through signs, wonders, miracles
and gifts, to the divine authority and truth of the message
preached.

With Accompanying Signs

This is in line with the commission which Jesus gave
to His disciples at the close of His earthly ministry, in
Mark 16:15, 17-18:

"...Go into all the world and preach the gospel to every creature...
"And these signs will follow (or accompany) *those who believe: In My name they will cast out demons; they will speak with new tongues;*
"they will take up serpents; and if they drink anything deadly, it will by no means hurt them; they will lay hands on the sick, and they will recover."

In these verses Jesus specifies five supernatural signs, ordained by God to accompany the preaching of the gospel message, and in this way to bear divine testimony to its truth.

These five signs may be briefly summarised as follows:

1, the ability to cast out demons;
2, the manifestation of speaking with new tongues (elsewhere called *other tongues*);
3, immunity to harm from snakes;
4, immunity to harm from poison in drink, or food;
5, the ability to minister healing to the sick by laying hands on them in the name of Jesus.

It should be emphasised that the introductory phrase used by Jesus, *in my name,* applies to each of the five signs that are specified. Each of them is effective only through faith in the name of Jesus.

It should also be pointed out that these five accompanying supernatural signs are not limited to any special class, or category of people. Jesus does not say: 'these signs will follow apostles'; or 'these signs will follow preachers'; or 'these signs will follow the early church.' He says: *these signs will follow those who believe.* All true believers have a right to expect that these supernatural signs will accompany and confirm their testimony, as, in obedience to Christ's command, they seek to proclaim the good news of the gospel to all men.

This was precisely how the first disciples interpreted and applied the commission of Jesus, as described in the next two verses of **Mark 16:19-20:**

So then, after the Lord had spoken to them, He was

received up into heaven, and sat down at the right hand of God.
And they went out and preached everywhere, the Lord working with them and confirming the word through the accompanying signs.

This supernatural testimony to the preaching of the disciples only came into full effect after the Lord Jesus had been received up into heaven and had taken His place at the Father's right hand. Thereafter the Lord Jesus worked with His disciples and confirmed their testimony not by His own bodily presence on earth, but through the presence and power of the Holy Spirit poured out upon them on the day of Pentecost. Thus it was the Holy Spirit who was actually responsible for the supernatural confirmation of the disciples' testimony. It is His special office to bear supernatural testimony to the truth of God's message.

We find this illustrated in the ministry both of Jesus, and of the disciples. Up to the time of His baptism by John in the river Jordan, there is no record that Jesus ever preached or performed a miracle. At the time of His baptism, the Holy Spirit descended upon Him from heaven in the form of a dove, and He was then led into the wilderness to be tempted for forty days by the devil. At the close of this period of temptation, Jesus immediately entered into His public preaching ministry, and for the next three and a half years His message and ministry were continuously attested by a great variety of miracles, signs and supernatural gifts.

That this supernatural testimony to His ministry was the work of the Holy Spirit, Jesus publicly declared in **Luke 4:18-19,** quoting a prophecy of Isaiah:

> *"The Spirit of the Lord is upon Me,*
> *Because He has anointed Me to preach the gospel to the poor.*
> *He has sent Me to heal the brokenhearted,*
> *To preach deliverance to the captives*
> *And recovery of sight to the blind,*
> *To set at liberty those who are oppressed,*
> *To preach the acceptable year of the Lord."*

Here Jesus very clearly ascribes to the anointing of the Holy Spirit upon Him both His preaching and the miracles of mercy and deliverance that accompanied it.

Again in **Matthew 12:28,** Jesus says:

"But if I cast out demons by the Spirit of God, surely the kingdom of God has come upon you."

Here Jesus directly attributes to the Holy Spirit the power that He possessed to cast out demons.

That the anointing of the Holy Spirit was responsible for the supernatural confirmation of Christ's ministry is stated also by the apostle Peter in the book of Acts.

In **Acts 2:22,** Peter speaks to the Jews concerning Jesus in the following terms:

"...Jesus of Nazareth, a man attested by God to you by miracles, wonders, and signs which God did through Him in your midst, as you yourselves also know..."

Peter indicates that one purpose of the miracles, wonders and signs in the ministry of Jesus was to approve, or to attest, the divine origin and authority of His ministry; and that it was God Himself who gave this testimony to the ministry of Jesus.

Again in **Acts 10:38,** Peter, speaking to Gentiles in the household of Cornelius, describes the ministry of Jesus in the following terms:

"...God anointed Jesus of Nazareth with the Holy Spirit and with power, who went about doing good and healing all who were oppressed by the devil, for God was with Him."

Here Peter specifically attributes the supernatural ministry and healing power of Jesus to the anointing of the Holy Spirit upon Him.

As it was in the ministry of Jesus Himself, so it was also in the ministry of His disciples. Before the day of Pentecost, there was a measure of the supernatural in their ministry.

Mark 6:12-13 gives the following description of the first twelve disciples whom Jesus sent out:

So they went out and preached that people should repent.

215

And they cast out many demons, and anointed with oil many who were sick, and healed them.

Again **Luke 10:17** describes the ministry of the seventy disciples whom Jesus sent out later:

Then the seventy returned with joy, saying, "Lord, even the demons are subject to us in Your name."

We see therefore that even during the earthly ministry of Jesus, His disciples shared in some measure in the supernatural aspect of that ministry towards the sick and the demon-possessed. But this would appear to be on a strictly limited scale, and merely an extension of the earthly ministry of Jesus through His close presence with them.

However, after the day of Pentecost the disciples immediately entered into a full supernatural ministry of their own, in which they were no longer dependent upon the bodily presence of Jesus with them on earth.

As a result of the descent of the Holy Spirit, one of the five supernatural signs promised by Jesus in **Mark 16** was immediately manifested: *they all began to speak with other* (or with new) *tongues.* The next chapter of Acts records the miraculous healing of the lame man at the beautiful gate.

Thereafter, the remainder of the book of Acts is an unbroken record of supernatural testimony by God, through the Holy Spirit, to the message and ministry of the disciples. This supernatural testimony to their ministry is summed up in the verse which we have already examined, in **Hebrews 2:4:**

...God also bearing witness both with signs and wonders, and with various miracles, and gifts of the Holy Spirit, according to His own will.

Of the five supernatural signs which Jesus promised in **Mark 16,** four are actually recorded as taking place in the book of Acts. The speaking with other, or new, tongues, was manifested on the day of Pentecost, and on various subsequent occasions. The healing of the sick, and the casting out of demons, were manifested in the ministry of Philip, of Paul, and, in fact, of all the apostles. Immunity to the bite of a poisonous snake was manifested in the experience of Paul on the island of Malta, recorded in **Acts 28:3-6.**

A modern record of these signs is contained in a small book entitled "Signs Following," published in the first half of the twentieth century. The author, William Burton, served for more than forty years as a missionary in the Belgian Congo.

In his book he considers each of the five signs in turn, and records several detailed instances, attested by his own observation and experience, in which each of these signs was manifested. In particular, he records instances of immunity, on the part of missionaries and evangelists, both to the poison of snakes, and also to other forms of poison, placed in their food or drink, by witch doctors opposed to the propagation of the gospel. Jesus promised that these signs would follow *those who believe* without any further limitations as to time, or place, or person.

In **John 14:12,** Jesus says:

> *"Most assuredly, I say to you, he who believes in Me,*
> *the works that I do he will do also; and greater works*
> *than these he will do, because I go to My Father."*

Notice the central part of this promise: *he who believes in Me, the works that I do he will do also...* The phrase *he who believes in Me* is absolutely general in its application. It means any true believer, anywhere. It is not limited to any special age, or place, or group or class of persons.

Exactly the same phrase, *he who believes in Me* is used by Jesus in **John 6:47:**

> *"Most assuredly, I say to you, he who believes in Me*
> *has everlasting life."*

It would be utterly illogical to give to this phrase a different meaning in these two passages where Jesus uses it. If the promise of everlasting life is open, without further limitation, to every true believer, then so is the promise, *the works that I do he will do also.*

How can it be possible that every believer can do the works that Jesus Himself did? The answer is given in the last part of **John 14:12,** where Jesus says: *because I go to My*

Father. A little further on, in verses **16** and **17** of the same chapter, Jesus says again:

"And I will pray the Father, and he will give you another Helper, that He may abide with you forever, even the Spirit of truth (that is, the Holy Spirit)..."

This statement here supplies the answer to the promise of verse **12.** It is the abiding presence of the Holy Spirit, sent down upon the believer from the presence of the Father, that enables him to do the work that Jesus did.

The same anointing of the Holy Spirit, resting upon the believer as it rested first upon Jesus Himself, leads the believer into the same type of supernatural ministry that Jesus entered into after the Holy Spirit came upon Him. This supernatural ministry is not due to any natural power or ability within the believer himself, but to the anointing of the Holy Spirit upon him.

Supernatural Revelation Demands Supernatural Confirmation

If we study the whole record of Scripture carefully, we find that this supernatural testimony to the truth of the gospel is in line with God's dealings with His believing people through all ages. Whenever God has committed truth to man by divine revelation and men have been willing to obey that truth, God on His side has always been willing to bear supernatural testimony to the truth which He reveals.

We find this at the very outset of human history, in the account of the offerings brought to God by Cain and Abel, as recorded in **Genesis 4:3-8.** These two different types of offerings are typical of two main patterns of religion through the subsequent history of man.

Cain brought of the fruit of the ground - but it was ground that had already come under God's curse, as recorded in **Genesis 3:17.** Cain's offering was the product of his own reason, and his own works. There was no revelation of God; no acknowledgment of sin, with its ensuing curse; no acknowledgment of the need for a sacrifice, to make propitiation for sin.

Abel brought of the firstlings of his flock, which he

offered in sacrifice. By this act he acknowledged the fact of sin and the need for a propitiatory sacrifice, with the shedding of blood. This came to him not through his own reason, but by divine revelation. His religion was based not on his own works, but on faith in God.

This is confirmed by **Hebrews 11:4:**

> *By faith Abel offered to God a more excellent sacrifice than Cain, through which he obtained witness that he was righteous, God testifying of his gifts...*

Because Abel believed and obeyed the revealed truth of God, God was pleased to bear supernatural testimony to his offering. Most commentators believe that the supernatural fire of God from heaven fell upon Abel's sacrifice, and consumed it.

On the other hand, God refused to give the testimony of His approval to the offering of Cain.

This is stated in **Genesis 4:4-5:**

> *...And the Lord respected Abel and his offering, but he did not respect Cain and his offering.*

In a similar way, ever since, God has always been pleased to give open, supernatural testimony to the truth which He reveals to man. In **Exodus 4,** we read that when God commissioned Moses to take His message of deliverance to the children of Israel in Egypt, God gave him three definite, supernatural signs, which were to accompany and to attest his message.

Leviticus 9:24 records that, when Moses and Aaron had completed their sacrifices to God in the tabernacle,

> *...fire came out from before the Lord and consumed the burnt offering and the fat on the altar. When all the people saw it, they shouted and fell on their faces.*

In **2 Chronicles 7:1,** we read that when Solomon had concluded his prayer at the dedication of the temple:

> *...fire came down from heaven and consumed the burnt offering and the sacrifices; and the glory of the Lord filled the temple.*

1 Kings 18:38-39 describes how the Lord confirmed

the message and the testimony of Elijah in his contest with the prophets of Baal:

> *Then the fire of the Lord fell and consumed the burnt sacrifice,* (that is, Elijah's sacrifice) *and the wood and the stones and the dust, and licked up the water that was in the trench.*
> *Now when all the people saw it, they fell on their faces; and they said "The Lord, He is God! The Lord, He is God!"*

The supernatural testimony of God to the message of the prophets did not end here with Elijah, but continued on through the ministry of Elisha, of Isaiah, of Ezekiel, of Daniel, and of many others.

In the New Testament, with the advent of the gospel, God's supernatural testimony to the truth of his Word, was not decreased, or withdrawn. On the contrary, it was greatly increased, and extended, both in the ministry of Jesus Himself, and in the subsequent ministry of the whole early church.

Throughout all ages, it has been the special office of the Holy Spirit to bear supernatural testimony to God's revealed truth, and to confirm the words of God's messengers. The more abundantly the Holy Spirit is poured out upon God's people, the more this supernatural testimony is strengthened and increased.

It has sometimes been suggested that a high degree of learning and education in God's ministers may render superfluous the special, supernatural testimony of the Holy Spirit. However, the outstanding example of the apostle Paul demonstrates that this is not correct. Intellectual learning, though useful on its own level, can never be a substitute for the supernatural power and ministry of the Holy Spirit.

It is clear that the apostle Paul was a man of high intellectual gifts and wide learning, both in the field of religion and also in the field of philosophy. Yet, in his presentation of the gospel, he deliberately renounced the appeal to his own learning, or the use of purely human forms of reason and argument.

This is clear from his own testimony, as given in **1 Corinthians 2:1-2** and **4-5**:

> *And I, brethren, when I came to you, did not come with excellence of speech or of wisdom declaring to you the testimony of God.*
> *For I determined not to know anything among you except Jesus Christ and Him crucified. I was with you in weakness, in fear, and in much trembling.*
> *And my speech and my preaching were not with persuasive words of human wisdom, but in demonstration of the Spirit and of power,*
> *that your faith should not be in the wisdom of men but in the power of God.*

Here we see that, in presenting the gospel message, Paul deliberately renounced what he calls *excellence of speech or of wisdom,* and again, *persuasive words of human wisdom.*

He implies that, had he chosen to use such forms of appeal as these, it was in his power to do so. But he renounced them in favour of an altogether different type of proof of the truth of his message. This other type of proof Paul describes as *the demonstration of the Spirit* (that is, the Holy Spirit) *and of power.*

Notice that word *demonstration.* This implies something open, public, and perceptible to the senses. The Holy Spirit did not work with the apostle Paul merely as an invisible, imperceptible influence. The presence and power of the Holy Spirit were openly demonstrated in his ministry.

Why did God appoint, and Paul approve, this supernatural form of testimony to the truth of the gospel message? Paul tells us the answer: *that your faith should not be in the wisdom of men but in the power of God.*

It is not God's purpose that the faith of His people should be based upon argument and proof on the level of purely human understanding. The only satisfactory foundation for the faith of each believer is in a direct personal experience of the power of the Holy Spirit in his own heart and life.

This is in line with what Paul says also in **Romans 15:18-19:**

> *For I will not dare to speak of any of those things which Christ has not accomplished through me, in word and deed, to make the Gentiles obedient -*
> *in mighty signs and wonders, by the power of the Spirit of God...*

Paul here refuses to base the authority of the gospel message, committed to him by God, upon any personal qualities of his own - such as his own natural talents, or learning. He states clearly that obedience to the gospel is not to be produced by any such qualities as these, but only by *mighty signs and wonders.* And these, he says, are the work of the Spirit of God - that is, the Holy Spirit.

Here, then, is one sovereign, unchanging office of the Holy Spirit - to bear testimony to the revealed truth of God by the open demonstration of supernatural power.

This supernatural testimony of the Holy Spirit commenced with Abel - the first believer, and also the first martyr, recorded in man's history after the fall. Nor will the Holy Spirit ever withdraw His supernatural testimony, so long as God has on earth a people who believe and obey the revealed truth of His Word.

For further reading in
THE FOUNDATION SERIES

Volume One

Book 1   FOUNDATION FOR FAITH

Establishes the place of Christ and the Scriptures in all valid Christian experience.

Book 2   REPENT AND BELIEVE

Man's first two steps to God - Repentance and Faith - fully analysed and related to modern living.

Volume Three

Book 5   LAYING ON OF HANDS

Presents Old Testament precedents and New Testament patterns for the Christian ministry of laying on of hands.

Book 6   RESURRECTION OF THE DEAD

Upon the stage of eternity the drama of the resurrection is unfolded in its successive phases and purposes.

Book 7   ETERNAL JUDGMENT

Vividly sets forth the scenes, the purposes and the principles of God's three great eternal judgments.

Other books by Derek Prince

Biography:
Appointment in Jerusalem

Guides to the Life of Faith:
Faith to Live By
How to Fast Successfully
Shaping History through Prayer and Fasting
The Grace of Yielding
The Marriage Covenant
Chords from David's Harp
God Is A Matchmaker

Systematic Bible Exposition:
The Last Word on the Middle East
Self-Study Bible Course